IN SEARCH OF EMMA

IN SEARCH
OF EMMA

How We Created Our Family

ARMANDO LUCAS CORREA

HarperOne
An Imprint of HarperCollinsPublishers

HarperCollins books may be purchased for educational, business, or sales promotional use. For information, please email the Special Markets Department at SPsales@harpercollins.com.

Originally published as *En busca de Emma* by HarperCollins Español

Translated from the Spanish by Cecilia Molinari

FIRST HARPERONE EDITION PUBLISHED IN 2021

Library of Congress Cataloging-in-Publication Data has been applied for.

ISBN 978-0-06-307081-3

21 22 23 24 25 BRR 10 9 8 7 6 5 4 3 2 1

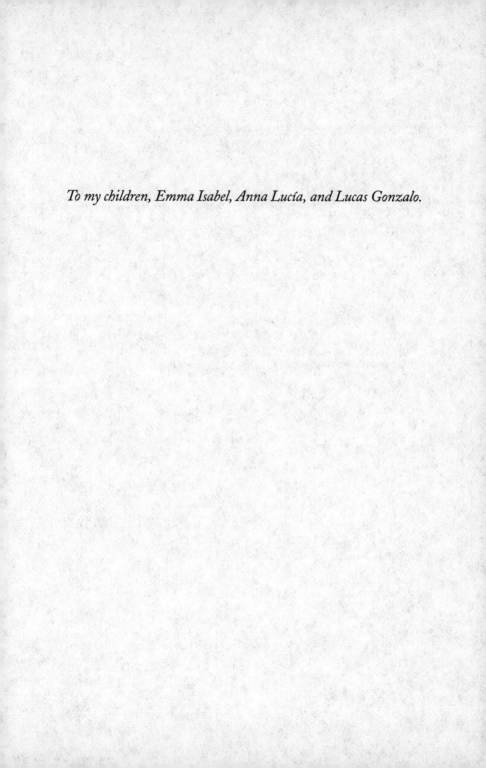

To my children, Emma Isabel, Anna Lucía, and Lucas Gonzalo.

With dreams, each man is given a small eternity.

—JORGE LUIS BORGES

In him was life, and that life was the light.

—THE GOSPEL OF JOHN

Whoever you are—I have always depended on the kindness of strangers.

—TENNESSEE WILLIAMS, *A Streetcar Named Desire*

CONTENTS

2005

THE ARRIVAL

New York
February 1, 2021

My dear Emma, Anna, and Lucas,

These pages are memory's artifice.

They are the silent conversation I began with you, Emma, on November 14, 2005, at 4:27 p.m., which then continued with you, Anna and Lucas, four years later, on December 13, in a dark hospital room in San Diego, California.

Emma, Anna, Lucas: this book is our framework.

I'll never forget the day you asked who your mother was, Emma. We'd just celebrated your third birthday. It was a time of princesses, clowns, and magic wands, remember?

You were holding the drawings you had made the previous night and said to me, "This is for your mom." I asked you who my mom was and you answered without hesitation, "Abuelita Niurca." And then I opened Pandora's box.

"And who is Papi Gonzalo's mom?"

"Abuelita Cuqui—she lives in Cuba," you answered, still engrossed in your precise lines. But after a brief pause, you asked the question we'd been anticipating: "And who is my mom?"

Gonzalo swallowed hard.

I replied, short of breath, carefully measuring each word, "You have two dads. Some children have a mom and a dad; others, two moms; others grow up with only one mom or one dad. There are even kids who are orphans; they have no mom or dad."

We remained silent, waiting. I counted the endless seconds.

"Would you like Mary to be your mom?" I suggested, referring to the woman who had carried you in her womb.

"No," you answered immediately.

"Your grandmother, your aunt? Do you want them to be your moms?"

"No," you repeated.

That night I began to assemble a small book with images of the day Papi and I traveled to San Diego for the first time to conceive you, our meeting with Mary and Karen, the day the doctors showed us the thirteen embryos, and when they transferred the one that would later become you. I also included photos of Mary during the pregnancy and on the day of your birth. A photo of you closed the album: you were dancing and playing in the snow, with sunglasses and a princess crown. I titled it "In Search of Emma."

Around that same time, you told us you wanted a little brother or sister. Since I tend to forget terrible moments, you led me to resume, without hesitation, the process of bringing another human being into the world. That's how you—Anna and Lucas—came into our lives two years after Emma's request.

The path has been filled with vicissitudes and accidents, but the three of you are our best creations. You came into this world to complete us.

Emma, your intelligence and sensitivity are our pride.

Anna, each night I long for our routine of taking stock of the day's events. Your wisdom and attentive eyes never cease to amaze me.

Lucas, I write down every one of your questions. Your ingenuousness and the level of your thought process make you special. You are a curious, noble, and kind boy.

Today, I observe the three of you walking by my side, almost reaching my height, and I'm thrilled to listen to your plans: one of you wants to be an aerospace engineer; the second, a vet; the other, a civil engineer. Each day I am more convinced that you are ready to face life, but I must admit that, despite seeing you happy, I can't help but feel an uncontrollable fear. I look back and can still hear the lurking voices.

Those who questioned why we brought you into the world.

Those who said you weren't our children.

Those who looked at you with pity.

Those who turned their backs on us.

Those who refused to baptize you.

Those who distanced themselves.

Those who said they would rather die than have two dads.

Since you were born, we have overcome each and every one of those battles together. Soon it will be your turn to defy them on your own.

I know that we've been happy, that we've given you the best education within our means, that you've been raised surrounded by love, and that we've prepared you to be compassionate toward ignorance. Never lower your heads. Look ahead, as far as you can, without stopping, without fear. The world belongs to you.

Once, you were our dream. Now, dear children, it's your turn to dream. Squeeze your eyes shut and you will see how, one day, those dreams will come true.

You are the proof.

Thank you for choosing us.

Papá and Papi

2000—2004

THE SEARCH

FEAR

To have one child, I have killed five.

That image haunted me for months. A cell, an embryo, a heartbeat. Every night I woke up startled: three, four, five embryos thrown into the abyss.

I prayed for one. Only one. The one who would have the strength to cling to the walls of an unknown uterus, with a heart that would ride on uninterrupted until one day, months later, it would burst into the world with a cry—the cry we all aim for.

First came fear. An eroding and paralyzing fear. Days, weeks, months of being terrified. The enemy of my endeavor was always lurking nearby. I was here and my potential children were there, on the other side of the country: from New York to California, the promised land. Never before had the East and West Coasts felt so distant. And strangers always on the prowl. Faceless voices with no soul. I heard phrases as instructions, words as orders. I had a whole army against me.

I made way for scrutiny. I had to go through the inquiring gaze of lawyers, doctors, nurses, psychologists, and social workers who analyzed every cell in my body. It seemed they were preparing to infiltrate my thoughts, even my dreams. I had to undergo every test imaginable; only then would I be allowed to contribute my 50 percent to the baby we would bring into the world. The other half would also be analyzed—not just the one contributing the precious cell, but much further back: one, two, three generations. All in search of perfection, of an ideal. There was no room for error.

I SUBMITTED TO that maelstrom only because, early on in my childhood, I had reached a decision: to become a father. I had just turned twenty when I got married—she was eighteen—and for two years, we avoided pregnancy at all costs. I didn't want my child to be born in Cuba, where we lived. We were very young and were both studying, but when our academic life ended, we decided to get a divorce. That was my first loss: as the opportunity to become a father "as God intended" slipped away, the possibilities of having a child dwindled.

Later, I met Gonzalo, and in 1991, we left Cuba for the United States. The idea of starting a family together had always been present in our relationship.

Adopting was an option, and I began in Ukraine—I still receive emails from adoption agencies there. At the time, Ukraine was one of the few countries with relatively flexible laws regarding the adoption of a child by a man of my age. Most countries offering possibilities of adoption required the candidates to be married heterosexual couples; several also had age limits. The process could take three to five years.

I gained access to orphanages in Romania and Russia as well as Ukraine. In all those countries I was presented with faces of children crammed into dislodged and dirty cribs. I corresponded both with other would-be parents, frustrated by the process, and with some who had overcome all obstacles and already had a baby under their roof.

Then we hit the main obstacle: in the state of Florida,

where we lived at the time, adoption was illegal for same-sex couples.

The deeper I got into the world of adoption, the more convinced I became that it was not the right path for me.

I wasn't ready for that whole inquiry process, which would persist even after having a baby: the constant home visits to evaluate the adopter's job as a father and, of course, the awful and enduring possibility that, due to some unusual bureaucratic decision, the child that you'd turned into your child, who now practically needs you to breathe, could be taken away in the blink of an eye.

Gonzalo and I moved to New York in 1997. I had been offered a job as lead writer at *People en Español* magazine, which increased my chances of being able to carry out my plan.

One day, the first press proof of an issue of *People* magazine arrived at my office, a privilege that stemmed from working for the same publishing group. In that issue, which would go on sale a few days later, I read for the first time a short piece that I would've considered science fiction if someone had mentioned it to me before.

In Phoenix, Arizona, a thirty-nine-year-old man had become a father through a gestational mother. The baby, a beautiful girl weighing more than eight pounds, was biologically and legally his, since the embryo that the gestational mother carried in her womb had been conceived with the sperm of the future father and the egg of a donor.

The man, who had been married for a short time and who for many years had struggled to accept his homosexuality, was determined to have a child. How? An ad from Surrogate Mothers, Inc., offering egg donation services and gestational mothers, had provided the solution; however, many of the candidates refused to work with him because he was a single man.

There were even two doctors who refused to do IVF (in vitro fertilization) because the man had no partner. His odyssey turned into the search for an egg donor and a gestational mother who would decide to help him. That's when his guardian angel appeared: a thirty-year-old woman who already had children of her own, and who agreed to start the process with him. How much did it cost? More than forty thousand dollars plus legal and medical expenses.

That day I found my way. I would have to overcome many obstacles, but I didn't care; it would be an exhausting process, but that didn't matter; it would cost a fortune—which I didn't have—but I'd find a solution.

From that day on, I was overcome by fear. And so, the battle began.

THE NEW MILLENNIUM

IT ALL BEGAN WITH a dream. I dreamed of my daughter on the last night of 1999. Gonzalo's family had gathered in northern Italy to ring in the millennium. They arrived from Cuba, Brazil, and Miami, and we came from New York. We all stayed in a small, late-1800s house in the city of Varese, thirty miles from Milan.

We toasted, we hugged, we celebrated the arrival of the twenty-first century, and I made no resolutions for the new year.

That night I went to bed and couldn't sleep. It was cold. Through an open window, I could see the dark, starless sky. I finally fell fast asleep right before dawn and had a dream. That night I saw my daughter. I didn't imagine her blonde or brunette, with blue or brown eyes. I dreamed of her in my arms, a newborn, her skin on my skin. I felt her, smelled her, caressed her, and fell asleep next to her. It was agonizing, but a pleasant kind of agony. I woke up flustered, short of breath, and with a racing pulse.

I'm not one to believe in dreams. I even tend to forget them.

My friend Norma Niurka calls me every time she has an extraordinary dream. She interprets them as visions, longings. She deciphers them, looks for explanations and connections with reality. Each element of every dream has a reason, in her view, and she narrates dreams to me as if they were plays: she gets excited and acts them out. She often believes her life is about to head in another direction, signaled by what her brain created while she was sleeping. Every time she finishes sharing one with me, at warp speed so that my attention doesn't wane, she asks, "You don't believe in dreams, right?"

And it's not that I don't *believe*. I just don't look for or find answers in dreams. I don't see them as premonitions, but rather as simple electrical slipups.

Oftentimes I can't even tell a nightmare from a dream. Both suffocate me. And, as with all other things that torment me, I place them in oblivion. Maybe that's why, when I wake up, I rarely remember my dreams.

But this time, the scenario was different.

A century was drawing to a close, I was far away from my family, and I had just turned forty. It was a dream I couldn't ignore.

The next day, a sense of complete calm washed over me. I felt relaxed, as if a huge weight had been lifted off my shoulders.

On the second day of the new year, we all took the train to Rome, which felt like a different city than the one I had traveled to on other occasions. I didn't feel the need to discover every corner, visit every museum, find scattered relics inside Renaissance churches, cross the Palatine Hill, feel the weight of the Arch of Constantine, lose myself in the labyrinths of the Colosseum or the mausoleum of Hadrian, contemplate the Sistine Chapel, or wander the streets of Trastevere. I just wanted to attend the first Latin mass of the new century in St. Peter's Basilica, which would take place that day, the second Sunday after Christmas, and would be dedicated to children.

Gonzalo toured the city with the others, while I got lost in a devout crowd from around the world, until I reached the altar, where one overcomes the fear of the void.

There, I knelt down, prayed for my daughter, and insistently asked to meet her. I explored every detail of the altar columns, looking for a sign. I gazed at Veronica's mantle and a piece of the cross's wood, relics that are on display only in sacred years. As commanded by the ritual, I crossed the great hall of the basilica and reached the formidable front door on the right, open only in jubilee years. I caressed the glossy knees of the crucified Jesus at the door, polished by the devotion of millions of pilgrims.

At the foot of the *Pietà*, protected by bulletproof glass, I lit a candle and prayed for my daughter under the reign of Pope John Paul II, the 264th pope.

I left the basilica in peace and joined our group in a tumultuous and cosmopolitan Rome, welcoming the new century amid the jubilee that marked the transition from the second to the third millennium of the Christian era. The city felt brighter, and I began to sense my daughter in every corner. She was my big secret. Nobody asked me what was going on, maybe because they noticed I was relaxed and happy.

THE RETURN TO New York was quick. On the plane, I tried to reproduce the dream over and over again. When I closed my eyes, I could still see my daughter in my arms.

Back in our Manhattan apartment, I began to chart the first steps to search for her.

I didn't want to, and couldn't, waste a second.

The apartment back then was small. We would have to move. Since it had increased in value, we could sell it and use the profit to finance the search process. If it didn't sell immediately, the room was large enough to fit a crib, some furniture, and the first few toys.

Now, years after meeting Emma, I try to draw her face as it

appeared in the dream, but I can't. I search that long-ago vision for her eyes, her tears, her smile, but I can't find them. I search for her thick hair and can't find it. Her hands, her small round face, her little feet. Nothing.

But I knew, even as I dreamed her, that she was my daughter, that we were physically and spiritually connected; and that day I promised I would move heaven and earth to bring her into the world.

ABSENT FATHER

FROM A VERY YOUNG age, I had a vague idea of how children were made. At home, no one ever told us they came from Paris, as one legend has it; and the story about the stork dropping babies in diapers down the chimney was too bucolic for a Caribbean island. No magic wand or immaculate conception. To have a child there had to be a man and a woman. And my family went into even more details: they told me that both had to be naked.

When I began school, things got complicated. My family pushed for me to start before the regular age—I never understood the advantage behind this—so, although I was the tallest in the class, I was always the youngest. That's where, through my older classmates, I came across other interpretations of how children were made. The first version, which I believed for a long time, had to do with a man releasing a liquid. So far, it seemed reasonable, but the person in charge of communicating this story assumed that the magic liquid was nothing more than sweat from the penis, which was exhausted from coming into contact with the vagina.

And so, I always assumed I was infertile: my penis did not sweat.

That's how early I began to worry about becoming a father.

I put my organ through extreme temperatures and particular gymnastics to make it distill at least one drop of sweat; however, not even the endless tropical summer was capable of making me fertile. That's why, from a very young age, I was certain that I could never be with women—and, consequently, never become a father.

Later, in a basic biology class, we were taught the process from a scientific standpoint, and then my trauma grew exponentially, because the information no longer came from a classmate but rather the teacher. Sweat was no longer the deciding factor now; I had to produce, inside of me, a much more complex liquid to make children. And so, regardless of how clearly it was explained, I still doubted my ability to inseminate; I didn't feel capable of releasing *any* type of magic fluid.

During my long journey to find Emma, and up until the moment I was shown my thirteen fertilized embryos, I continued to doubt my fertility.

Today, I not only know how babies are made, but I can unravel the process almost on a cellular level. I ended up creating my own stork.

Perhaps that yearning to be a dad had something to do with not having had a paternal presence while growing up. My parents divorced when I was only two and a half years old. My mom remarried, and the stepfather I had from a very young age was nothing more than a pathetic stranger whom I've banished into oblivion, as I usually do with anything I find unpleasant.

Although I was raised in a matriarchy that marked my life—my grandmother, mother, sister, aunts, cousins—the imposing presence of my maternal grandfather was a source of great inspiration to me. My abuelo Lalo, an elegant man, always donning his fedora, was well-mannered, passionate about history, and business-savvy. Given his weak eyesight, affected by diabetes, he would dictate his letters to friends and children to us with vigorous nineteenth-century rhetoric. At night, he'd count his small fortune, lend money to friends, and strategize his finances. Once I learned how to add and subtract, I became a kind of accountant for him, grouping together bills and cleaning his antique silver coins. My grandfather was my idol—until he took me to an empty room of what used to be Río Bar, a business he'd built in Guantánamo and lost after the triumph of the revolution. My grandfather, whom I had already passed in height, drew near me and, with great precaution, said, "It's better to be a thief, a murderer, than a fag." I started to shake but remained silent. When he turned away, I went home, straight to my room, trembling, and burst into shame-fueled tears. I was thirteen years old.

MEANWHILE, MY FATHER, whom I encountered only sporadically during my childhood and youth, had formed a new family. By the time Emma joined us, he had lived with his second wife for more than fifty years and had three daughters, whom I rarely called my sisters—not out of spite or jealousy but due to lack of habit. Each of my sisters had two children, so my daughter would be just another grandchild to him. She'd be his youngest one.

After not seeing him for over two decades, I began searching for my father about a year after Emma's birth so that she could meet him. I reunited with him for her. Although I doubted a two-year-old girl could etch in her memory an encounter that would last only a couple of months, she would at least, as the years went by, have a photo of herself with her grandfather. An absent grandfather, but at least one with a name and a face.

Inviting him to visit me was a great odyssey and, like many

of my plans, it began in secret. The utopia lasted more than a year, until he managed to get a visa to enter the United States.

The first time I picked him up at the airport, I felt like I was meeting a stranger. Wearing a pair of old and extremely heavy glasses that gave him the appearance of an elder man, he exited customs and crossed the airport's waiting area with a frightened look on his face. I felt no connection with him, but I hugged him as if we'd seen each other just yesterday. He was taken aback, and I sensed that he attempted to establish some distance. When I got near him for a photo and placed my arm on his shoulder, his body tensed up as if not wanting me to get too close.

My father is a man of few words. Discreet, he avoids problems. I think he uses the same resource I do: evade anything that could distract me from my path, and even more so if that distraction involves drama. We agree on that.

Two days after his arrival, my father began to change. His face was rejuvenated, his cheeks turned rosy, a new haircut gave him a certain air of dignity and made him look younger. I watched him enjoy his silence, lose himself in his leisure, delighting in the opportunities it provided. He didn't know how to gratefully acknowledge the time he recovered by our side.

But as my father drew closer to me, I pulled away. A distance that was, paradoxically, an honest sign of trust.

We spoke about the past, the rare times we'd met. About his paternal family, whom he rarely saw, his parents, his grandparents, his childhood. He recalled youthful moments with my mom, who received him on this visit with familiar warmth.

It was fun to see them together, in a relationship that seemed more like that of siblings who hadn't seen each other for a few years than husband and wife who had stopped living together five decades ago. I often tried to imagine what my mom thought when she saw him, strong and healthy, still dedicated to his job;

an exemplary husband and father to a family he formed after divorcing her. Did she wonder what life would've been like with him?

When talking with my half-sisters in Cuba during that time, they were surprised by our father's reactions. He'd always been devoted to them; close yet also distant. He wasn't affectionate, they'd never seen him cry; but in our reunion, we saw him shed tears, express deep admiration for his lost children—my sister and me—and relish every moment, knowing that it would soon come to an end.

The best thing about our reunion was not reproaching each other about what we did or didn't do throughout all those years. I saw myself in him and he saw himself in me, and I think that was satisfying enough. Observing him and feeling that I too could age with the same dignity gave me peace.

My father is a good father to his daughters. He wasn't a bad father to my sister and me, simply an absent one. Someone we always wanted to be close to but couldn't due to circumstances that eluded us. I never imagined that becoming a dad would allow me to reunite with my own father, but that's what happened. Now we know him better and love him, thanks to Emma.

I WANT TO be the father I never had for my children. Be there when they are born, see them grow inch by inch. See them cry and laugh for the first time, teach them how to crawl and walk. I doubt my father recalls my childhood the way he does his daughters'. He remembers the day they were born, their birthdays, beach vacations, the time they cut their hair extra-short.

Since I dreamed about my daughter, I've visualized her year by year, in every stage of her life. On her way to school, the day she graduates from high school, her first weeks in college, her first love, her wedding day. I will be there, nearby, for whatever she needs.

That's why I brought her into the world, that's why I searched for her: so that she could be happy, be loved, and grow up surrounded by people who love her.

She will stumble across obstacles and be strong; she will overcome difficulties; she will fall down and get back up, cry, and then laugh again. But she will always know that I am there for her, when she cries or when she laughs.

She will also encounter those who question how I brought her into the world, who say I denied her the chance of having a mother; they will even mention God. But she will know how to explain it to them, since she's here because of God's will. Because God *gives* life, He does not *take* it. God favors love and is against intolerance. The most perfect embryo can be created in a lab, but, as the doctor who helped me conceive my children put it, for an embryo to become a baby, that's in God's hands. Emma and her future siblings exist because of nothing more than an undeniable act of creation.

Slowly, they too will understand this and learn how to defend themselves. And they will answer those who question them with a smile.

I NEVER DOUBTED what I was doing, not even for a second, because I knew I wasn't alone. My search didn't defy any law of nature. On the contrary, my children are light, they are life. And life is the work of nature.

THE FIRST AGENCY

JUNE 2000

Every time I have to make a momentous decision, such as moving from Miami to New York, returning to Miami, accepting a new job, or even committing to writing a book, I turn to my friend Mirta Ojito. I joke with her when I say I'm following in her footsteps.

She was the one who hired me at the Miami newspaper *El Nuevo Herald* as a news department assistant. I later became a reporter, and when she left for the *New York Times*, she recommended me as a writer to the editor of *People en Español*, an entertainment magazine that was just starting out. Her recommendation paid off, so Gonzalo and I left for New York, home to that magazine. A few years later, Mirta returned to Miami to write a book, and a while later I followed her and worked from there, still with *People en Español*. When Mirta went back to New York, I unintentionally had to return as well.

So, after reading the article about the man who had his child through a gestational mother, I called her. Back then, Mirta had two young children, and she was moved by my plan. Since she knew me, she knew I would make it happen. Mirta always has an answer, at least the one I need.

"My New York gynecologist had his son like that," she said. "His wife couldn't have children, so they went to an agency in Oregon. Now they're the parents of a baby."

Of course, I immediately called Mirta's gynecologist, who replied unenthusiastically but gave me all the information I asked for. His child had been born only ten months earlier, and he was hoping to repeat the procedure to have a second one.

That was my first agency: Thorsen's Surrogate Foundation, in Portland, Oregon. I had no idea where that was, if the laws allowed surrogacy in that state or what percentage of babies were born from gestational mothers, but I jumped in headfirst.

New York
June 16, 2000

Dear Dr. Sampson:

I am writing to you today in hope that you can help me fulfill my lifelong dream of becoming a father. I have done extensive research and my options are limited. My answer lies in gestational surrogacy. Science and technology have made the process of fertilizing an egg in a laboratory a reality for me.

Now all I need is for you to help me find a wonderful, generous, and dedicated woman who would be willing to bring this dream to life.

Included is all the necessary information to begin the process.

I hope to hear from you soon.

Sincerely,
Armando

My first conversation with Dr. Sampson was harrowing. The barrage of medical terms and procedures, as well as the real possibility of having a baby, left me on the brink of unconsciousness. The odds of becoming the father of a baby through in vitro fertilization were 25 percent.

Gestational surrogacy—which entails an egg donor, the father's sperm, and a gestational mother (sometimes referred to as a carrier)—would further reduce my chances. In gestational surrogacy, the woman selected to carry the baby for nine months cannot be the same one who donates the egg, which is fertilized in a laboratory (in vitro) with sperm selected from the father's donation. The resulting embryo is transferred to the gestational mother's previously prepared uterus. The fact that the gestational mother is *not* the baby's biological mother is an advantage in this assisted reproduction technique, as it prevents more emotional complications than those already implicit in the process.

Dr. Sampson advised I instead go with traditional surrogacy, where the surrogate mother is the same one who provides the egg. In that case, the father's sperm is used to fertilize the egg through artificial insemination. The surrogate mother's ovaries are stimulated with medications that induce ovulation. The body naturally produces only one egg during each monthly cycle. With this induction procedure, several eggs are developed in the same cycle. The semen is then prepared in the lab: among millions of sperm, those with optimal morphology and motility are selected. Insemination is carried out at the doctor's office, without anesthesia, and the surrogate mother needs to remain at rest for only several minutes after the procedure.

This process worried me, since the surrogate mother would have to deliver a baby that she had carried in her womb for nine months, and it would be her biological child as well as mine. In the case of a *gestational* mother, the baby inside her would *not* be hers, so giving the baby to its genetic and legal father on delivery day would be less traumatic. Or so I thought.

In both cases, before the pregnancy a legal contract would be drafted, by which the surrogate mother would relinquish the embryo, whether created in a lab or inside of her with sperm extracted from a semen donation. In the best-case scenario, as the future father, I would be the sole responsible, legal, and biological father of the baby; the gestational mother, if I went that route, would relinquish her rights before a judge during her pregnancy, at which time I would be granted parental authority for the unborn child.

The assumption was that I would be at the birth, that the baby would fall under my custody once born, and that I would appear as the father on the birth certificate. Depending on the state, the name of the carrier might or might not appear on the certificate. Later, with legal help, the name of the gestational mother could be removed from the certificate so that only mine would remain.

In some states, surrogacy requires adoption, with the adoption procedures stipulated by the hospital and the state where the baby is born. In Oregon, the baby's biological father—that would be me—would have to adopt the child. Apparently, that was my only option in that state, which filled me with even more uncertainty.

In both types of surrogacy, the documents containing the names of the carrier and egg donor could remain legally sealed, and thus could be consulted only with a judge's authorization.

I was facing a big dilemma with regard to the traditional surrogacy method: How could a mother "abandon" a newborn baby, which she had carried in her womb and which belonged to her on a cellular level, regardless of contract terms? How could a gestational mother, knowing that the baby was in no way hers, and aware that she would have to hand it over, deal with the hormonal upheaval caused by pregnancy and childbirth?

Oregon is a small state with just four million residents. Unlike neighboring California, a state with cases that legally supported surrogacy, in Oregon there were at that time no laws related to the use or payment of a gestational mother. In other states, such as Kentucky, surrogacy was prohibited if it involved paying for a surrogate or gestational mother to waive her rights to the baby. Regardless, Kentucky had surrogacy agencies, and that law had yet to be applied. In some states, surrogacy was recognized and state intervention was minimal, so several agencies could conduct their practice unhindered. There were also states where the gestational or surrogate mother's contract had no validity. Outside of the United States, there were countries where gestational surrogacy had legal protection, such as New Zealand, South Africa, Canada, and India. In Spain, the legal agreement between the gestational mother and the future parents was still not recognized. In Argentina, a committee evaluated case by case for approval. In Brazil, there were no laws regulating such a procedure. In the United Kingdom, it was allowed as long as it didn't involve a profit. In Israel, it was accepted as long as the gestational mother was single and the couple that hired her was married. Its approval is still being debated in France. In China and Italy, it is forbidden.

At least in Oregon there were no laws *condemning* surrogacy, so it was a real possibility for me.

Once I had practically decided to go through a traditional surrogacy process—I believed that it all came down to who the surrogate mother would be—I began the arduous process of writing and compiling documents, biographies, and essays to convince a surrogate mother to accept me as a parent who was searching for a baby.

To protect myself, I locked myself in total secrecy, keeping even my friend Mirta in the dark about my progress. Something told me that traditional surrogacy was not the right way, but up until then, it seemed to be my only path. I was living in a state of constant distress; I began to have difficulty sleeping and my fear returned.

The doctor recommended a sperm analysis to measure my level of fertility, especially since I had never fathered a child. My head started to spin with the real possibilities of male infertility: I could be suffering from asthenospermia, a condition that involves reduced motility of sperm, or oligospermia, which consists of excessively low sperm count in ejaculation; or even worse, azoospermia, the complete absence of sperm in the semen.

To eliminate my uncertainty and really begin the procedure, or at least the signing of contracts phase, the doctor recommended I go to my primary care physician (PCP) with an extensive list of blood tests. We needed to exclude, he said, any possibility of venereal or sexually transmitted diseases and HIV (human immunodeficiency virus), as well as another series of viruses that I had never even heard of, and more well-known diseases such as hepatitis and hematologic deficiencies.

My stress levels skyrocketed. I constantly wondered, *How did I get here? How far will all this scrutiny go?* My child would be born in Oregon to a mother who had decided to abandon it. And I thought, *It will be an undesired child*, although I knew it would be more than loved by Gonzalo and me and those around us. But it would have the adopted child syndrome, always in desperate search for the mother or father to whom it's connected genetically, and who decided to abandon it to a stranger. In my case, I would be the real father, so I took comfort in knowing that the syndrome would affect my child by only 50 percent. That was my therapy.

Nevertheless, even with my uncertainty in full swing, I began to imagine my baby, trying to give it a face, but it was impossible. And the terror intensified when I began to close in on the stratospheric costs of the entire process.

I'd have to get rid of the apartment. Leave Manhattan. Start a new life far, far away from the city. But first, I would have to go into debt. Find money where I could, resort to credit cards, loans with exorbitant interests.

I was coming to an unknown crossroads, trusting strangers that I knew only through the internet or sporadic phone calls. Faceless names I had to trust with my eyes closed. And trust I did.

That summer came to an end and I braced myself for the arrival of fall. If I found the surrogate mother and we inseminated her in the next two months, my daughter or son would be with me in less than a year. I couldn't believe it. I still didn't see myself as a father. It was one thing to dream of it and another to see myself in that role, but the journey had begun. I would have my baby the following summer. And he or she would be born in Oregon.

What are Oregon natives like? Is the state Republican or Democrat? All these questions prompted me to begin an investigative process (had it ever ended?). How many electoral votes do Oregonians get? Who are their senators? Has any US president come from Oregon? What writers and other famous people are from Oregon?

In what hospital would my baby be born? Would I have to adopt it, or would it be legally mine from the moment it was born? That's when I began to see the first signs, portents. One was Oregon's fascinating motto: "She flies with her own wings" (*Alis volat propriis*). Second: Oregon is the only state in the country that has an official state nut, the hazelnut, which is my favorite. Ninety-nine percent of the country's hazelnuts are grown there.

I went back to the agency's website, but it was a bit limited. It didn't provide detailed information on staff or how many babies had been born through surrogate mothers or egg donors. Of course, it did list the process's estimated costs, without clarifying that those expenses could skyrocket into eternity.

The best thing about that entire interlude of analysis and research was that I'd taken the first steps. I was already immersed in the process, and I began to understand how these types of agencies work. This understanding was based on my reading and on phone calls, mind you. I hadn't yet progressed beyond my desk.

In short, as I understood it, a surrogacy agency is like a hospital. Before entering, you must be admitted, and it's important to get an initial medical checkup. Upon your admission, agency personnel treat you as if you were sick. They first set out to discover the gravity of your condition, whether it's operable, and whether, in the end, the surgeon will agree to take you to the operating room. More than a future father, you are a patient, and they begin to compile your medical history.

Worse still, in addition to being a patient who is difficult to diagnose, you also become a guinea pig. No one knows what will come out of the process—if the results will be positive or negative—and, in fact, you have absolutely no idea if an agency is telling the truth or misleading you. Complicating matters, no insurance covers this type of care. All things considered, you are a kind of homeless person begging for medical attention; and even if you have some money saved, it will never be enough.

I couldn't find any photos of the agency, so I used my imagination. I envisioned it as a small hospital office with a friendly receptionist behind a glass window. If you rang the bell, the receptionist would open the window and smile, and you would try to sniff out what's on the other side. I also imagined a complex lab filled with graduated cylinders, test tubes, nickel-coated steel tanks, and groups of doctors absorbed in electron microscopes. The lobby would have photos of babies on the walls, and of pregnant women smiling at men who together contemplated the size of their belly. And of course, I imagined the doctor who would be manipulating the embryos in a white long-sleeved coat, with the face of an illustrious professor wearing glasses and a busy expression, sighing over the answer he gives you, the one you've been waiting for. The doctor would be in his sixties, with more than thirty years of experience and, to his credit, the creation of more than a thousand children.

But in reality, I hadn't met him yet. I had only heard his calm and soft voice trying to convince me that my best way to have a baby was through artificially inseminating the surrogate mother. Traditional surrogacy.

DIANA

JULY 2000

DIANA IS THIRTY YEARS old. She was born in California and lives in Oregon. She is married, has children, and now wants to be a surrogate mother. Why? She gave up one of her babies when she was very young, and her experience was beyond positive. She assures me that she could do it again because, although it wasn't easy, she was moved by the reaction of the future parents with their new children. She wants to help those who want to make their dreams of becoming parents come true.

Diana chose me. She works, but she wants to study computer science and web design. She has a beautiful smile and a motherly face. Her eyes are crystal blue and her hair is light brown. She is short and carries a few extra pounds. It's clear she struggles with her weight. She is a healthy woman who doesn't wear glasses or contact lenses, has never had her teeth fixed, and has never had surgery. She is a happy woman. She likes to dance, likes to sew, and is fascinated by crafts. She also likes to visit vineyards. According to her, she has a great sense of humor, is responsible, and has a good heart. She also adds that she's outgoing.

She has had no problem conceiving. Her pregnancies have gone smoothly, she's carried them to term, and they all ended in natural deliveries. Her periods are regular, every twenty-eight days, and she's on the pill. Her pelvic exams are normal. She has never had any sexually transmitted diseases. She hasn't had rubella, either. Her health status? Excellent.

Diana doesn't suffer from depression, nor do any of her relatives. She's never been under psychological or psychiatric treatment. The only medications she takes are for headaches or the occasional toothache. She has never used illegal drugs. She has never smoked and doesn't drink alcoholic beverages—"only occasionally, about once a month," she clarifies.

Her children have not suffered and do not currently suffer from any serious illness, and there is no asthma, alcoholism, blindness, diabetes, hepatitis, mononucleosis, epilepsy, allergies, arthritis, unusual bleeding, obesity, polio, tuberculosis, or high blood pressure in her family history. Her weak spot is her skin, which is very sensitive and easily irritated.

Her mother recently died of cancer at the age of sixty-nine. Her father died at forty-five of a stroke. Diana's sisters are alive and well. Her paternal grandmother died at eighty-seven; her grandfather at ninety. She doesn't know her maternal grandparents.

Her husband, she says, supports all the decisions she makes and is happy that she wants to be a surrogate mother. Her children are too young to understand the step she's taking. Her job also has no issue with her being a surrogate mother. She can count on her friends at all times.

She anticipates that, when handing over the baby after the delivery, she will be a little sad, but that she will also feel very happy for the future parents.

In the photos she emails me, her children look happy. The family has breakfast at home every morning, she says. Her husband drops the children off at the nursery and she picks them up at the end of the day. She cooks dinner every night and allows the children to watch TV for a couple of hours.

The house, located in a family-filled neighborhood, is small. It has only one bedroom. The children sleep in the living room. The kitchen is spacious, and Diana says it's her family's favorite place to hang out. She likes to cook. Her kids love her apple pie and freshly baked chocolate chip cookies.

On Saturdays they usually go to the park together and then, in the afternoon, head to a movie. On Sundays, after mass, they have lunch at a family restaurant. Diana will use the money she receives as a surrogate mother, around twenty thousand dollars, to study computer science. She wants to give her children a better future.

It's decided, then: Diana will be the woman who will carry my future child in her womb. She will also be the baby's biological mother. She won't be at all opposed to letting it go, to handing the baby over to me so that it can become my child. This will be my biological and legal child, and Diana says it would greatly please her to see me happy and help fulfill my dream.

And yet . . . what I can't figure out, even though I try to convince myself this plan will work, is how Diana will be able to let go of a child that she will not only carry in her womb but also procreate. How will she tell her children that she's giving one of their siblings up for adoption? Diana has done it before (though not through deliberate surrogacy), and I'm sure she could do it again, but I still try to understand her, think like her. And I don't succeed; I just don't get it. I can't imagine Diana as the biological mother of my child, the woman who would give the child half of its chromosomes, half of its genetic code. A woman who gave her first child up for adoption. Although, to be fair, she would also be the woman who would donate her egg to create my child, and would carry it in her womb so that I could then have that baby in my life.

ON MY WAY from the office to the subway, I see a potential surrogate mother in every female I come across. I look at hips, which must be wide; breasts, voluminous; abdomens, powerful—and I can't stop thinking about what Diana's like.

As I walk into a subway car, I see a thirty-something woman sitting in front of me, pregnant, discreetly straightening her tight-fitting blouse. I rest my eyes on each of her gestures, try to guess exactly how old she is, whether her pregnancy was desired, if this is her first child, if she had symptoms during the first trimester, if she will be able to give birth or will have to undergo a C-section. The woman responds uncomfortably to my scrutiny: only then do I realize that I haven't taken my eyes off her.

We reach my stop and I leave the station convinced that Diana will be the mother of my child. After looking at her photos so often, I feel as if I know her; she has become a member of the family, someone whom I will soon be very close to.

"Diana, thanks for choosing me," I say.

She hugs me tenderly and holds me tight. I reiterate my thanks and pull back, looking at her intensely. Her belly has grown; she caresses it and smiles.

"This is your child; what I'm carrying in here belongs to you." Her voice is warm. She says goodbye and walks away. She turns around, still smiling, and waves. As she walks farther and farther away, her figure begins to blur, but it's still distinguishable even as it merges into the horizon.

"Diana, thank you," I say again. And I know, though she's just a smudge in the distance, that she is smiling and also grateful. I don't want her to disappear; I try to follow her footsteps so that she doesn't evaporate.

I lose sight of her and come to my senses.

I was daydreaming. It was a sweet dream.

INFERTILE

AUGUST 2000

I'M JUST ANOTHER PATIENT and I have to wait. In the reception area, a boy takes refuge behind his mother's legs as she tries to comfort him. An old man slowly attempts to fill out long forms. A woman talks incessantly on the phone, switching from one call to another with contagious anxiety.

There are no windows. The office doors are closed. It's hot. A phone rings and nobody answers. I feel ignored, like that desperate patient who's calling with no success. Finally, I hear my name and go to the first window. Without making eye contact, the woman extends her hand for me to give her my doctor's test orders. Her face tenses up; she opens her eyes and looks at me for the first time, as if trying to figure out why the hell someone would need so many tests, 50 percent of which are related to sexually transmitted diseases. A door opens and light comes in from a window in the next room. I try to look through the window to avoid the sense of confinement. The bleary-eyed woman prepares a label for each test, hands them to me, and tells me to step into the room at the right.

"For this one," she adds, pointing to the test's name with her index finger, "you'll have to go to this other lab," and she points her finger again.

"This one" is the sperm test, which she apparently didn't dare name. And the "other lab" she referred to is a specialized clinic, where I imagine there will be several dark rooms in which lonely men, fearing an answer that could question their virility, must donate their sperm—in other words, masturbate—for an expert to read what they may not want to hear.

A skilled phlebotomist finds my vein on the first try and begins to draw blood as if I'd signed up to participate in a donation drive. One, two, three, four test tubes . . . and then I stop counting.

Somewhat sore and affected by the decreased amount of blood in my body, I go back past the woman who first helped me. I can feel her following me with her eyes until I leave the premises, perhaps imagining what I will soon have to do at the "other lab." I feel weaker, more vulnerable.

I take one of the buses that cross Manhattan through the heart of Central Park, and in the Upper East Side, on the first floor of an elegant building, I find the lab that the woman didn't dare name.

I hand my lab order to the receptionist who makes me fill out a long form and then tells me to go to a bathroom that's more like a cell with a toilet and a sink. I find an old *Playboy* magazine and a shelf stacked with sterile plastic jars sealed with green labels on which I must write my name, the date, and my Social Security number. I feel like a prisoner, sentenced to death.

The donation takes a few minutes. When I hand in the sample, the receptionist places it in a plastic box while avoiding eye contact.

The results?

"Your doctor will have them next week," she replies, still not looking at me. I am a ghost.

THAT TEST IS proof that I'm already immersed in the process of becoming a father. I've donated my sperm and will get the results by Monday, or no later than Tuesday. I'm happy to be moving ahead, yet I can't help thinking about all the negative possibilities. It's an involuntary exercise I routinely do to prepare myself for the most dreadful news. Oftentimes the actual outcome has nothing to do with the script that I've orchestrated.

My biggest concern is not having sperm, although, if I do, there's a possibility that none will have reached ejaculation alive, I think, to spur myself on.

But a specialist could rescue a live one from my testicles, at least one. After all, only one would be needed to fertilize the precious egg and have my daughter.

However, if we decide to work with Diana, it will be a traditional surrogacy. In that case, retrieving more than one sperm will be indispensable.

How many? A lot. The quality? Optimal. They would have to navigate full speed ahead and be strong and combative, so as to break the zona pellucida and penetrate the egg. Only one would be necessary to fertilize it, but that one brave and intrepid sperm would have to swim alongside thousands of colleagues before reaching its destination. And its head would have to be perfect. As well as its tail.

I'm heading into a long weekend. In a couple of days, my fate will be decided. We all have a fate.

IT'S MONDAY AND I call my primary care doctor's secretary. She confirms that the results are in, but the doctor can't see me until Wednesday. Two more days? "Can't you tell me if the results are okay?" I plead. "If there's anything I should worry about?" Probably tired of having to dole out explanations, she cuts my anxiety short with a biting phrase: "I can't read results. I'm not a doctor. If I were a doctor, I wouldn't be answering the phone. You can speak to him on Wednesday. Be here by three p.m."

What's the reasoning behind calling someone your "primary care physician" if you have absolutely no access to him when you need him most, if you can't consult with him, have his cell phone number at your fingertips, and feel that *he's* the one answering all of his patients' calls rather than a clumsy intruder?

I should have feigned an emergency, I think, and insisted that he get on the line; then I could have demanded that he read the results to me. Or I should have shown up at the office and sat in the claustrophobic waiting room until he finished treating each of that day's elderly patients.

His office is near my office. Instead of calling a secretary who is not a doctor—which is why she answers the phone—why didn't I wait for him outside his office so that he could see my despair up close and take pity on me? I just need him to say, "Everything is fine. Don't worry. Come on Wednesday at three and we'll review the details." Or have him face me with pity and, with his arm around my shoulder, say, "It's not what we were expecting, but we'll figure it out. Come see me on Wednesday."

The results of my analysis are there, in a small office inside a majestic art deco building with gilded gates protected by a burly doorman who keeps intruders like me—who want to reach a doctor who doesn't see anyone without an appointment—at bay.

There is nothing to do but wait two more days.

FOR SOME, WINTER is the most terrible and inhumane season in
New York. For me, the worst season is summer. I grew up in the
tropics and have lived in Miami, but nothing comes close to the
unpleasantness of New York heat.

The city stinks in the summer. Subway stations have poor
ventilation. Tourists invade the streets, and the moodiness of
those who live on the tiny island crammed with skyscrapers in-
variably prevails.

Everyone is fed up—at least those who have no home in the
Hamptons, or can't seek refuge on the French Riviera or in a
Tuscan villa. My PCP is one of them. He has to work summers.
He sweats profusely, even in an air-conditioned environment.

He treats his patients as if he were scolding them, "What the
hell did you do now? What do you want me to do?" And you feel
guilty. Guilty of a cold, or a piercing headache, or your irritated
skin, or the sinusitis that doesn't let you sleep. *You* are the only
cause of your own miseries. Solve them. What do you expect from
a doctor who sweats, has to work every summer, and has no vacation home?

Sometimes my PCP realizes he's crossing a line and then
softens his tone; first he attacks and then he gives me a hand.
But "giving a hand" is just a figure of speech.

I sit on the exam table and wait like a good patient for my
doctor to enter the office, which looks more like a closet. My
medical record is on the door, waiting for his experienced
hand to grab it, for him to skim it and communicate the results I've been awaiting through sleepless nights. I lean in to
read the parts of the human body as shown on a faded poster
by the small window. I've spent fifteen minutes waiting, sitting on the exam table. It's now three fifteen. That was my

time of birth. Finally, my doctor shows up, sweaty and tired as always. I smile tentatively. There are no greetings. He takes my medical history and quickly flips through the pages. It's impossible: he doesn't have enough time to read that many numbers and codes, which only he can decipher and not the secretary, because that's why she is a secretary and only answers the phone.

"This is bad. There are issues," he tells me, seemingly without giving it a second thought. As if, without being a doctor, I could have read my blood or semen from the moment it was drawn. I was the only one to blame—who else?—for my results having issues.

Do I have a venereal disease? Am I infected with a deadly virus?

The doctor, expressionless, reviews page after page. He stands up, calls the secretary, and orders her to cancel the next patient's appointment.

What about me? Is he planning to leave me like this, like a dying man who isn't worth showing the slightest sign of compassion?

He looks me in the face. Though he says nothing, it's as if he were yelling, "Did you really not know this, dumbass?"

His silence feels like an eternity. I ask nothing, but rather wait for him to deign to explain the crime that I will have to pay for throughout my life. What is my life sentence?

In an instant, everything has crumbled. Me, a sick man, a fool, trying to become a father. A man who now has to fight God knows what, one who had selected a good woman and hoped she would donate her egg and her womb to carry his plan to term.

Now I will have to apologize to Diana, because clearly everything will have to stop.

How can I have you, Emma, if I can't even take care of myself? Me, a man who until this day had considered himself healthy.

"Given this result, I don't think you can have children," my doctor finally decrees. "Your sperm is no good. You are infertile."

THE VOID

SEPTEMBER 2000

E VERY TIME I FACE an interview, I'm overcome by a fear of the void. Even if I've prepared the night before, even if I've come up with all the questions, written them down or recorded them in my mind, I never know what I'll encounter. The uneasiness stems from being unable to predict the interviewee's mood, if we'll have chemistry, how far I'll be able to go with my questions, and whether the person across from me—who has been trained to not go off-script from what they're "supposed" to respond, who has built an image hoping no one will alter it—will answer honestly in the end.

One of my strategies is to begin with questions that the interviewee expects, slowly picking out elements in common and using them to guide the conversation toward more intimate and honest places, so much so that at times it seems more like a confession. But some interviewees are experts at answering what you haven't asked. Others conclude with set phrases that the audience doesn't want to hear, and there are even those who spend the entire interview repeating one or two convoluted and triumphalist answers that, with luck, could be used. In the presence of the subject, it's almost always possible to get an interesting idea, which may stem from the interview preparation, the setting where the conversation takes place, the personnel who take care of the interviewee, or even his or her body language. And, of course, there are interviews that end up being good and others that are bad. The bad ones, I always forget.

I TAKE A plane, arrive in Miami, and before checking in at the hotel, I head over to the Univision studios in Doral. Waiting for me is María Celeste Arrarás, one of the main anchors of the country's number-one Hispanic TV network. She will soon be heading in to makeup before presenting the news on *Primer impacto*.

María Celeste is excited. She's planning to write about her recent trip to Russia. She's the mother of Julián, a three-year-old boy, is five months pregnant with a girl, and has just adopted another boy, Vadim, at the Rayito de Sol orphanage, which is two hours away from Moscow. The first time María Celeste saw Vadim was on the internet. They emailed her a photo of the baby; he was dressed in pink and weighed twenty pounds. Later, she and her husband, Manny, visited him. Vadim was wearing a T-shirt with the number six on it. His clothes were dirty and reeked of a musty stench. He shared his room with eleven other babies and wasn't used to seeing men. Now María Celeste's dream of having three children will be fulfilled. She's also happy because she's going to save a baby from misery.

I leave Miami moved by María Celeste's story and fly to Mexico. The actor Saúl Lizaso is waiting for me at the Casino Español, an imposing colonial-era building in the center of Mexico City where *El derecho de nacer*, the new version of a telenovela classic, is in the middle of being filmed. Dressed in a period costume, with a stately air, Saúl walks down the halls of the casino, which serves as his home in the TV series.

In that instant I feel like another character in the drama. At a distance, I see the protagonist, Kate del Castillo, cry because her character doesn't know who her mother really is. She's been abandoned. I feel pathetic. Nothing is real.

When "Cut!" is yelled out, Saúl sets aside his starchy character, approaches me, and gives me a hug. He invites me to his dressing room in a windowless trailer with clothes hanging everywhere. He's happy. Not only is he one of the highest-paid actors at Televisa, the Spanish-language soap opera empire, but fourteen months ago he became a father. His daughter, Paula, is his pride and joy. He tells me he changes her diapers, bottle-feeds her, and even wakes up at dawn to comfort her when she cries. Saúl stars in a successful telenovela and has been selected by *People en Español* magazine as 2000's sexiest man alive, but he emphasizes that his most important role to date is being a father.

I fly back to New York, and the next day I'm sent to Clara Barton Elementary School in the Bronx, where a group of fifth-graders is waiting for me. Eleven-year-old Elvin, who lives with his parents in a South Bronx apartment, is the captain of a team that pretends to trade stocks. They "invested" one hundred thousand dollars, and in about ten weeks made a thirty-five-thousand-dollar profit. The children, mostly Hispanic, have become famous overnight. In a year, they could've become millionaires, if they hadn't been investing imaginary money in a hypothetical stock market. Before heading out to play baseball, Elvin checks the *New York Times* business pages to see how his investments are doing and, together with his friends, decides where to invest next. Their parents have no idea where this investor's talent came from, but they are extremely proud.

Back at my office, on the thirty-sixth floor of the Time and

Life Building, I begin to transcribe the three stories—María Celeste, Saúl, the Bronx children—missing the usual adrenaline that my work evokes.

I'm still carrying my test result, folded in four, in my pocket. I haven't been able to speak to anyone. And I haven't dared to call the agency and cancel my project with Diana. It's as if this test business never happened.

On my desk, I spread out the photos of María Celeste with Vadim in her arms. In one, she looks at him tenderly. In another, she places him in a crib. In a third, Manny holds him in the air and María Celeste smiles at him, beaming with happiness. Vadim looks at her as if he knows his martyrdom has come to an end. Now he's going to have a home and María Celeste will have another son.

I remove the sperm analysis from my pocket and try to decode the numbers expressed in millions, the percentages, the data on morphology and motility. I don't understand a thing. I just know that those figures express that I'm not fit to have a child. That I will never be able to fertilize the embryo that Diana would've donated to me; that none of my sperm could cross the intricate path to Diana's fresh, healthy, and perfect egg, pierce its walls, and share its genetic code with hers to begin the creation of my daughter.

That is my fate. It was written, and I hadn't known it.

I look at Vadim's cute little face and think of all the children waiting for kind and brave parents who will dare to rescue them. Vadim is a lucky boy. María Celeste is a lucky woman. That is their fate. Mine is laid out on the piece of paper before me, and it has just hit me like a resounding slap in the face.

Do I have a genetic flaw, or am I somehow to blame for my misfortune? Could it have been the extreme temperatures I put my testicles through to make them sweat during my adolescence? Or my obsession with losing weight and subjecting myself to grueling steam baths? Could long hours with a laptop on my lap have affected my ability to produce healthy sperm?

"With this result, there's no chance of artificial insemination," is the Oregon agency doctor's reply. "I don't think it'll be possible for us to fertilize an egg."

Goodbye, Diana. Goodbye, Oregon. I will no longer have to travel to or get to know Portland. My daughter will no longer be born on the other side of the country. Apparently, she will no longer be born.

A BROKEN HEART

APRIL 2002

I**T'S MIDNIGHT AND GONZALO** is sleeping. I finish a bowl of green tea ice cream and fall asleep too. At three in the morning, an unyielding pain in the pit of my stomach jolts me awake. I go to the kitchen and drink a glass of milk, but the pain continues. I go to the bathroom, but it doesn't simmer down. My jaw begins to go numb and the pain spreads to my right arm. I start doing stretching exercises. I sit down, walk, lie down again. It's six in the morning by this point, and the pain has intensified. Gonzalo wakes up to find me in a state of utter despair. We make a lay diagnosis of heartburn and he heads to the pharmacy to buy Zantac. I take a pill, the pain goes away almost instantly, and I fall asleep.

Later, from my office, I call my friend Maria in Miami and tell her about my strange pain. Was it just a dream? Maria is my conscience.

"You should call your doctor," she advises.

My new PCP is a Mexican Harvard graduate who has an office in the Upper West Side's legendary Oliver Cromwell Building, across from the Dakota. Unlike my previous doctor, he seems to have all the time in the world for me. I explain what happened.

"If you took a Zantac and the pain went away, it must have been indigestion," he says reassuringly. "Come see me tomorrow."

The next day, my friendly PCP listens to my heart, checks my vitals, and does an EKG. He carefully analyzes the curves on the long strip of graph paper and recommends that I see a cardiologist. He calls the specialist's office and sets up an urgent appointment for me.

Every face in the new waiting room looks tired. The patients are in their sixties. What happened to me? Did my heart fail me? I don't smoke, I don't drink, I don't do drugs . . .

The cardiologist does an echocardiogram, takes some blood, and has me come back the following day to examine the state of my arteries.

When I return to my PCP's office for the results, he tries, with his usual patience, to calm me down.

"I have good news and bad news. Which do you want to hear first?"

The bad, of course.

"You had a small heart attack. We can tell because the blood enzymes are somewhat altered. The good news is that there was no damage. You don't have any clots in your system."

Just what I need. My sperm is useless and my heart has decided that it no longer wants to work.

My fate is sealed. I return, as directed, to the cardiologist, who greets me with a youthful good mood.

"Who would have guessed it, huh? But let's find out what happened," he says, trying to calm me down. Radioactive imaging, a stress electrocardiogram, and X-rays follow.

My mother is alarmed and wants to take the first flight from Miami to New York, but I don't allow it.

"With the results we have, there are two options," explains the cardiologist. "Either I put you on drugs for life to keep the arteries unclogged, or we do a cardiac catheterization. We'd use that latter approach to find out whether there's a need to operate—that is, to unclog any possible obstruction—and to see exactly what happened to you. The tests we've run so far have an inevitable margin of error; they can't confirm anything."

The medications he mentions can keep the heart healthy for a few years, he explains, but they can also start to damage the liver or kidneys. I feel like a disabled person.

Why me, if no one in my family has heart disease, my parents are alive and healthy, and my grandparents died at a very old age?

Cardiac catheterization would tell us my situation's exact level of severity. For Eduardo, a work colleague, a simple yet constant pain in his elbow led to a biventricular pacemaker after a catheterization revealed that he had several blocked arteries. So, in open-heart surgery, Eduardo had to endure having veins transplanted from his legs to his weak heart.

Will I need a pacemaker? How clogged will my veins be?

I choose catheterization, and my mother, hearing of it, arrives in New York the following day.

I look like a dying man. I walk slowly and cautiously, avoiding any stimulus so as not to agitate my heart, which apparently decided to stop for a few seconds. I avoid eating any type of fat and try to stay in bed most of the time.

At the hospital, I walk over to the preoperative gurney after signing documents that note the dangers of catheterization. I could die instantly and the doctors would not be held responsible.

As they insert the needle into my groin through which they will introduce a catheter that will flood my arteries with a contrasting medium, tears roll down my cheeks. I can't stop crying, and the nurse at my side seems surprised to see my emotional distress.

"Easy," he says. "I get this done every year, and on two occasions I've had a couple of arteries unclogged. It's nothing," he adds in an attempt to comfort me.

He doesn't know that this is the end of a project. I'm not crying about what *might* happen to me, but about what *will no longer* happen to me.

They take me to the operating room while my mother and Gonzalo wait in a family area.

The doctor inserts the catheter and explains that when the liquid enters the coronary circulation, I will feel cold and my heart will beat faster. If he finds a blocked coronary artery, he will use an inflatable balloon to unclog it.

Up above, several black-and-white screens display my insides. The doctor points out my arteries to his team, detailing each step. The liquid begins to stain the ramifications that reach the heart, which has not stopped beating, at least not on the screen. The pumping is amplified; it sounds to me as if I had already died and were watching the movie of my life. The doctor explains to his assistants—not to me—that my arteries are not only unclogged but healthy and wide; they have more than enough space for my blood to circulate well.

"What about my heart attack?" I ask, incredulous.

"I don't think you had one."

I don't think? Is it that hard to say outright, "You didn't have a heart attack"?

Another decision is now imminent. I have two options: they either stitch up the incision that was made to insert the catheter, which would mean a slower recovery, or they insert a type of plug, with which my recovery would be immediate. However, the plug is an experimental procedure that could cause a clot to form, which in turn could reach the lungs, brain, or heart.

"What do you recommend?" I ask the cardiologist.

He answers without hesitation. "Definitely the plug."

Soon after, I exit the operating room with the plug.

The doctor informs Gonzalo and my mother that I'm well, but in the postoperative consultation with the cardiologist, doubts reemerge.

"Well, you don't have anything wrong that I can see. What seemed like a heart attack could have been a spasm, a sudden change in temperature. It could also have been the result of a virus or bacterium; but to find *that* out, we would have to do a heart biopsy, an even more invasive procedure."

I say no. No more testing. To this day, I still don't know what happened to me.

The PCP, who somehow feels guilty for not having seen me immediately when I called him about my first symptoms, has become even more patient with me.

"You didn't tell me you were planning to have a child," he says when I mention it in conversation.

I tell him about the Oregon agency, Diana, my previous doctor, and the ill-fated semen analysis. Perhaps taking pity on me because of my heart episode, he ventures a glimmer of hope. He explains that each donation is different, since sperm is renewed every three months. He suggests I visit a urologist and undergo a more detailed exam before making a final decision. Sometimes the cause can be testicular varicoceles in the testicles, which can be fixed with a simple surgery.

But before I begin to worry about my testicles, I have to recover from my heart scare. It hasn't been an easy time.

Excited about this newfound possibility, I start looking into gestational mother agencies in New York, New Jersey, San

Francisco, Los Angeles, La Jolla, San Diego, and Boston, requesting information and catalogs. And so begins a long thread of electronic correspondence with unknown women who are offering their services as gestational mothers and egg donors.

After all of these signs, my search has turned into a purpose. Yet I'm not ready to undergo further studies to find answers that I don't want to hear.

ANGEL OF THE WATERS

MAY 2003

Joan Lunden, fifty-two-year-old former host of ABC's *Good Morning America*, is waiting for her twins to be born. Except that she isn't pregnant: a gestational mother carries babies in her womb, created with the sperm of Joan's forty-four-year-old husband and the eggs of a donor. Joan is not infertile. She has three daughters—fifteen, twenty, and twenty-two years old—from a previous marriage. Her current husband, owner of a children's summer camp, has no children. She decided to turn to a gestational mother to have their children, who will be born in June.

I've been closely following Joan's story, and it gives me hope. Still, it takes me the better part of a year before I go back to my PCP in the spring of 2004 and tell him it's time to take action. He orders a testicular exam with a urologist—the exam he suggested when he told me about testicular varicoceles on my previous visit—and the results come back normal.

"Your varicoceles are minimal; there's no need to operate. They aren't the cause of infertility here either," my PCP explains.

The urologist, for his part, had also requested a complete analysis of my sperm and, during my appointment, without preamble, he enlightens me as to the results:

"To have a child, all your specialist needs is *one* healthy sperm. And you have millions. The agency will know how to select the best one, so don't worry; go ahead and start the process."

I'm ecstatic. I don't know whether to thank him, hug him, laugh, or call everyone and tell them I'm going to have a baby.

Within a second, I conjure up all the mistakes I've made. Who recommended my first PCP to me, and why—and how could I have accepted that doctor's verdict as if it were God's word? Why didn't I question it or have the determination to seek a second opinion? Why did I accept that I was an infertile man, if there was no logical, hereditary, or accidental reason to support it?

I've been trying to find signs, but sometimes we stumble upon them, they stop or even hit us, and yet we insist on ignoring them. It's easier to discover—and we tend to be more open to receiving—the signs that we *want* to find than those that actually exist. When signs surprise us or imply a detour from our desired path, we usually cut across them as if they were transparent.

The signs, I should have seen the signs. But which ones? Well, for starters, it's *never* good to go with the first opinion. Maybe I simply wasn't ready yet financially to take such a radical step toward making the legal and genetic commitment to having a child with a surrogate mother.

Was Gonzalo the one who hadn't wanted to do it? No, he was beyond convinced; it was something we had discussed for years. It was our project. I had recently graduated from college when we met in Cuba and moved in together, and together we managed to leave Cuba with an invitation from a university in

New York. Together we moved to Miami and created a home. And now the time had come to become parents, to have a real family.

As THESE QUESTIONS filled my mind, I began to feel like I was coming out of a four-year hiatus. I was climbing out of a void, one I perhaps never would have emerged from if it hadn't been for my savior of a doctor, the patient PCP; or thanks to my supposed heart attack, or the divine grace of a doctor who told me that only one—one brave sperm—was enough to fertilize the egg with which my child's life would begin to take shape.

Didn't I know this? Hadn't I read it?

Did I feel hatred? I don't remember anymore, since I always try to forget everything that causes me pain. Did I regret having squandered so much time? Four years had passed; four wasted years. Trust is not possible. You always have to doubt. No one has a definitive answer.

Now, in the aftermath, I feel absolutely drained. I feel unable to call my mother, text my sister, or run to see Gonzalo at his work and interrupt him by shouting, "It's time to seriously search for our child!"

On my way home, I cross Central Park. I want to walk, take time to process the good news. I reach the Bethesda Terrace and Fountain, in the heart of the largest public garden on the island, and stop to gaze at the tourists and the tireless runners, the lake, the buildings that tower over Central Park West. No view is more relaxing in the park than that peaceful lake. I'm not sure if it's the tree-lined paths, the calm water, or the angel presiding over the fountain. The statue is known as *Angel of the Waters*, designed in the mid-nineteenth century by Emma Stebbins.

Emma. Gonzalo loves the name Emma. It's short, has a round sound, and is pronounced the same in English and Spanish.

Perhaps our daughter will be named Emma, like the protagonist of *Madame Bovary*, the novel I read when I was ten years old in Havana, and which I still reread with pleasure. I buy different editions, different translations—Flaubert is an obsession. Emma Bovary is an obsession.

I go down to the terrace, walk around the fountain, and stop to observe every detail of the bronze angel, including the lily in its left hand. At the base of the angel, four cherubs represent peace, health, purity, and moderation.

Feeling more settled now, and attuned, I think again of that doctor whose name I've forgotten. But I don't remember him in his dark and narrow office. No. I remember him one night in a modest restaurant in New York's theater district, while Gonzalo, my friend Cristina, and I had dinner. From the opposite end of the restaurant, the doctor greeted us with a wave; we smiled, and he sent us a bottle of Italian wine as a gift with the waiter. The harvest year was printed on the bottle's label in large font: 2000. We had a couple of drinks and thanked him on our way out.

That's the only scene that comes to mind now, and it's my last memory of him.

THE SECOND AGENCY

JANUARY 2004

O N THE FLIGHT FROM New York to Los Angeles, a woman in her sixties sits down next to me and remarks on the beautiful day. The moment someone greets me and comments on something—whether it's the weather or the book I'm reading or how full the plane is—I know I've just landed a talkative flight partner. When traveling, I prefer silence. I like to read, think, or sleep. I'm not enthusiastic about engaging in an inevitably conventional dialogue, least of all with a stranger.

It's her first trip to the West Coast to visit Hollywood, explains my chatterbox of a partner. She will be reunited with her son, daughter-in-law, and granddaughter, who have been living in San Francisco for two years. Although they've visited her in the New York suburb she calls home, it's the first time she's decided to fly to the opposite end of the country.

By the sounds of this conversation, I assume I won't be able to read my book or get organized before landing in Los Angeles. Fortunately, the woman fast-forwards to the question that, according to my calculations, she would leave for last:

"And you? Why are you going to Los Angeles?"

Never have I been more explicit.

"I have an appointment at Growing Generations, an agency that provides services around gestational mothers and egg donors, to start the process of having a child. Tomorrow I must donate my sperm; then they'll analyze it, store it, and with the egg donor already located, they'll prepare an embryo. The embryo will then be transferred to the womb of a gestational mother and, by the grace of God, in nine months I will be a father." I smile at her.

The woman smiles back, wide-eyed, and doesn't speak to me again for the remainder of the five-hour flight.

AND WHAT I told my seatmate is what happened—or at least the first part.

The decision to choose Growing Generations had been quite simple. It's one of the largest and oldest agencies in the country. It was cofounded by a woman who had a son with her partner—another woman. The other owner is a lawyer specializing in assisted fertility, who had her children with the help of a gestational mother.

The agency's offices weren't hidden in a corner of the city, like those of some companies, or inside the owner's house, like others. Growing Generations stood in the heart of Los Angeles, on one of its best known and most luxurious thoroughfares, Wilshire Boulevard. I discovered that they had never been sued and, most important, they worked with any type of family, be they married couples, single women or men, or same-sex couples.

Before traveling to meet them, and after my first phone call, I received an email from Teo, one of the agency's executives, with a well-structured itinerary for my visit. First, I had to fill out the typical and extensive questionnaire designed for future parents. That time it was easier because I used the one I'd given the Oregon agency as a model. The questionnaire actually had to be in the agency's possession before my trip. On the day of the appointment, first I had to go to a lab to donate my sperm, which the agency would then analyze and freeze for possible use later.

An hour and a half after that, I would be greeted by members of the Growing Generations team, including its president, who would answer all my questions.

Instructions for the lab donation were also included in the email. If the method chosen was in vitro fertilization of a gestational mother, the semen could be used immediately. If the process was to be traditional surrogacy, where the surrogate mother is artificially inseminated, the doctor might impose a quarantine on the semen. An underlined warning appeared in all caps: for the donation it was necessary to abstain from sexual intercourse or masturbation for no more than five and no fewer than three days.

Ready for the procedure and having met all the requirements, I arrived at the lab. To my surprise, it wasn't like what I was used to in New York. The reception room, with sand-colored sofas and a predominance of wood and glass, was set up like a spa. There was indirect lighting and everyone present appeared to be relaxed, as if waiting for a pleasant massage. Nobody greeted each other, however; and there was no eye contact.

The nurse ushered me into a large private room where, to my surprise, there were a variety of videos that catered to all sexual preferences. I received a plastic cup with the label and warning that "when donating the specimen, be extremely careful to keep the inside of the bottle sterile." And so I got to work, taking care not to contaminate the enchanted vessel with foreign elements.

Filled with the conviction that this donation—in which they would surely find millions of healthy sperm—would provide the brave one or ones that would fertilize the egg, I marched on, upright, ready to conquer Growing Generations.

Having developed a preconceived notion of these agencies, this one wasn't what I expected. I thought I'd find a space designed to look like a nursery, full of women telling men how brave they are for having made the decision to become fathers through a gestational mother. I thought that we'd talk about my work, that agency personnel would share anecdotes, that they'd show me photos of newborn children who had come into existence with the help of the agency; I thought we'd be interrupted by emergency calls every ten minutes because someone had gone into labor.

Instead, I felt like I was in a bank—there was no one but me—ready to open an important account or sign a lease for a car that, after sealing the deal, I wouldn't be able to get rid of for at least a couple of years.

First, I was met by the person who coordinates the search for gestational mothers, and then the person in charge of the egg bank. Someone gave me a tour of different rooms divided into small cubicles with computers where, after signing my contract, I could browse the database to find the gestational mother and the egg donor who would help me have my child.

Stuart, one of the executives, praised my shoes, and then it was time to meet the president, I imagine everyone must have noticed my jitters. Gail had had her daughter through artificial insemination. Her partner's brother had been the sperm donor, I learned.

With a gentle voice, she struck me as a relaxed, even maternal woman, with traces of childbirth on her body. She knew how to treat me, how to help me, because she knew "everything you had to go through to get to this point." And she insisted that I had come to the right place, the ideal agency to have my child.

Then I met with Teo to discuss an aspect that we had so far ignored in all previous conversations: finances. Along with the signed contract, I had to deposit a ninety-thousand-dollar check. My face must have reflected my astonishment. Not because I was unaware of how expensive the procedure was, but because the agency required the entire payment up front, which was beyond my means.

Teo added that I could see the database first, but that I would very likely have to spend time on a waiting list before matching with a gestational mother, as well as with an egg donor.

Before I said goodbye, they gave me a list of clients who had become parents and were satisfied with the agency's services, so that I could reach out to them and listen to their experiences, in case I had any questions.

I left Los Angeles in a panic.

Back on the plane, I anxiously searched for someone who would need a conversational partner during the outbound journey. It was imperative that I find someone who would talk, someone who wouldn't stop talking, so I wouldn't have to think about how to come up with ninety thousand dollars in less than a week. But this time my traveling companion was so lost in thought that he didn't even look up when I asked for permission to take my seat. It was a long flight, and I was unable to read, sleep, or even close my eyes.

But I had an inkling that I had just positioned the first grain of sand to have you, Emma.

When I arrived in New York, I was convinced that there was no season more beautiful than spring.

Rebecca, one of our editors at the magazine, announced that she was pregnant with twins.

THE ENDLESS PROJECT

FEBRUARY 2004

I AM OBSESSED WITH PROJECTS. My friend Herman sometimes greets me by asking, "What project are you working on today?"

Maybe that's why I've survived for so long at an entertainment magazine. Every month is like starting over: searching for a topic, selecting a cover, testing various images until the final one wins out at the editing table. Before the pages even go to print, I'm already deep into a new project for the next month, or for the following one, or for the one that will end the year that has just begun.

I enjoy the process more than the results of a project. If I intend to buy a computer, a camera, or a TV, I spend days, weeks, and even months researching what the market has to offer. Once I bought a shaver and, after studying all its possibilities and trying it out for a couple of days, returned it. I tried another brand and, a few days later, returned it to the store too. I repeated the process with yet another one. The irony is that I tried and returned them all, only to end up rebuying the first one I had purchased. Gonzalo, of course, doesn't get it; he gives up and leaves me be with my obsessions.

The day I decided to get a dog in New York, my research led me to an English bulldog. I found a beautiful, white three-month-old in Tennessee. Choosing him, having him shipped, and picking him up at the JFK Airport cargo area was an exhausting process. Herman warned me, "A dog is not a shaver; once you get one, you can't return it." And I didn't return him. Paco, the English bulldog, lived with us for six years. When Herman realized that the search for Emma had finally begun, he repeated the same phrase to me.

But a child is an endless project, which begins the same day you decide to have him or her. Every day is a surprise, an investigation, an evolution. Each stage puts you face to face with the unknown. It involves several subprojects that converge at one point. A circle with no beginning or end.

Because Gonzalo and I had decided not to tell anyone about our earlier efforts with the Oregon agency until we knew something for sure, this ongoing project was going to be news to a lot of people. The first person I told was my mother, over the phone. "We've decided that we're going to try to have a child," I said. Silence. A few seconds that seemed eternal. I heard her take a deep breath and reply, "Ay, *mijo*." I'm not sure if it was because she knew this was a project that might not materialize, because it was clear that I didn't know what I was getting myself into, or because children are always a headache.

"Talk to your sister," she recommended.

Sahily, my sister, was more direct. "You're crazy," she said. "Are you sure?"

Neither of them yet knew that, since 2000, I had been in a process that had merely been interrupted, and that for the last few years I had been living with the bitter feeling of failure. I had just found my way, and felt that the obstacles, at least those that involved me, had been overcome. Maybe my sister thought of herself, pregnant at twenty-five and then cheated on, separated, and divorced. In that split second, she probably relived the terrible labor pains, the arrival of Fabián, the infrared incubator to treat his jaundice, and his newborn asthma attacks. Or perhaps she also thought of her struggle to escape with him from Cuba and join us in Miami, the sleepless nights to make him study, or the battles at school. But Fabián is a good and healthy boy who loves her as unconditionally as she loves him; they're a unit, constantly exchanging love and support.

In January 2020, Fabián would make her a grandmother to Catherine, a beautiful baby.

I cut the conversation short with my sister without searching for reasons or whys to help answer anyone's questions. I did the same with Herman, who apparently thought we had lost our minds. Perhaps he couldn't imagine a child in our minimalist, monochromatic living room, which didn't display the slightest sign of potential parenthood, much less that we would survive the chaos of colors, plastic toys, and weeping children.

When I mentioned the plan to my nephew, Fabián, he was the first to refer to the future. "What are you going to tell your children in a few years? Are you going to tell them how they were conceived?"

He spoke in the plural. And now I was the frightened one. *The children?*

But he quickly added, "Great, I'm going to have a cousin!"

That night, my mother called me with resolve, surprising me with a categorical phrase: "We are going to support you in whatever you decide."

Even so, I felt a pinch of fear in her voice, slight overtones of pity and distrust in the face of the unknown. It must have been difficult for her to imagine a process that I explained with a single sentence but that neither she, nor even I, fully understood.

At least I didn't feel rejected. I had exposed my secret and could now openly speak about what was to come.

We decided to call Cuba to speak with Esther, Gonzalo's mother, who had no idea about the process we had gotten ourselves into. When she heard her son, she was happy. I was on the other phone, anxious. Esther began to tell us about her visits to the doctor, her sick neighbor, the medicines she needed, her next trip to Italy. She wouldn't stop talking, wouldn't give us a chance to tell her why we were calling.

Finally, Gonzalo interrupted her. "Mami, we're going to have a baby. It's going to be a test-tube baby. A woman is going to carry the embryo in her womb."

Silence. And a few seconds later, "Have you lost your minds?"

Why did everyone associate the birth of our baby with insanity?

"The situation is very bad in Cuba. Things are not good here," Esther ventured.

"But we don't live in Cuba. We live in New York, we work in New York, and yes, we want to have a child," we explained.

"So when is the baby going to be born?"

"We don't know, Esther. In a year, a year and a half, two? We've already started the process, and everything is going to be fine. We'll find a wonderful gestational mother who will happily give us the baby who belongs to us," I replied.

"Well, if you've already made up your minds . . . but things there are also bad. It's bad everywhere. Think about it . . ."

"We really have thought this through, Mami," Gonzalo said. "We've had four years to process the idea. What you've just heard in less than a minute took us years to understand. Yes, we want to have a child, and you're going to adore him or her."

I wondered how Esther felt after hanging up the phone.

On my desk, I once again opened every dossier of the agencies I had contacted during the last four years: those with the most prestige; the state that provided the greatest legal protection for prospective parents in the surrogacy process; what I should keep in mind when selecting an agency—whether it was created by former gestational mothers, by lawyers specializing in surrogacy, or by physicians specializing in assisted reproduction. Some worked only with married couples. Others did not accept single men, but they did accept single women. Others did not work with gay men. Still others specialized only in gays.

Too much information. With every passing second, I grew more convinced that I had made the right decision, that the trip to Los Angeles hadn't been in vain. I was unwilling to face the possibility of rejection because I wasn't married or because of my sexual preference.

I went to bed and tried to sleep. Tomorrow would be another day, with new projects that would arrive; and whether they were carried out or not, they would be transformed . . .

Only this one would endure, the endless project.

EVERYTHING CHANGES

MARCH 2004

I BOUGHT MY APARTMENT ON Manhattan's Upper West Side in the summer of 2001, the worst year in the history of the city that never sleeps. It was no-frills, but it had everything you could dream of to live on this island: a good location, space, and light.

The same year I made this purchase, sure that it was an excellent investment, a terrorist act destroyed the Twin Towers. That day, everything changed: the city and those of us who lived in it.

Years later, the absence of the towers is the indelible reminder of that disastrous September 11. But we survived, and so did the city. Our investment too—our only possession.

By 2004, all I had to do to take the next step was put the apartment up for sale. *This endeavor may easily take two, three, or even—at most—four months*, I thought. I had to find the ninety thousand dollars to begin the process.

Another possibility, if I didn't want to wait, was to start off with my credit cards, which would allow me to withdraw cash. I wasn't too concerned about the cards' interest rate because, when the apartment sold, I would pay off the debt.

Another option was to research which bank would give me a line of credit against the value of the apartment—and again, when it sold, I could pay off the loan immediately.

Although the latter was the most practical alternative, it could take more time, not due to the bank's response or the value that the apartment had acquired in those three years, but because we lived in a co-op, where a board had to approve all financial transactions related to property value.

And so began, on the one hand, my navigation of the overwhelming bureaucratic bank labyrinth, and on the other, my corresponding feelings of panic.

Teo's voice echoed in my mind, "Ninety thousand dollars." It took him only two or three seconds to pronounce that sum. When I first heard it, I asked him to repeat the figure; so much money couldn't be covered in a few seconds. I didn't dare say the number out loud myself, but all those zeros reverberated in my mind.

As I signed the legal documents to surgically remove the ninety thousand dollars from the apartment, I felt as if the house that had accommodated us all that time, the place we called home, was about to undergo a complicated operation that would strip her of one of her vital organs.

Astoundingly, I was about to give ninety thousand dollars to a man with whom I'd spent barely an hour. That man would place the money in the coffers of an agency that was committing to but not guaranteeing—a phrase they repeated with discreet insistence—that I would become a father.

What would they do when they received the check and my signature, which guaranteed that I would work with them? Perhaps their impassive faces would light up and they'd go out to celebrate that one more fool had fallen into their trap.

I imagined myself with a lifetime debt of ninety thousand

dollars (I couldn't erase the figure from my brain)—and no baby. I'd be tied up in a project that would amount to nothing. Amid that chaos, I received a call from the agency that drove me to continue searching for money.

"The sperm test results are fine," the agency representative said. "We can work with what we have." He also assured me that the president was confident we could sign the contract.

Fine? How fine? I wanted to see those results, make copies of them, read them every night so that no figure escaped me.

He then sent the analysis of the results, more detailed than any other I had seen before. The donation had been made at 9:12 a.m. (it's always recommended that it be done as early as possible), after three days of abstinence. The color was clear and the liquefaction time was fifteen minutes. The seminal pH, ejaculation volume, and sperm concentration were within normal parameters. There were 95.76 million sperm, with 60 percent motility. The report went on to describe details of the sperm's hyperactivity and progressive velocity. In the area of morphology, the results were not as promising: some sperm had amorphous heads, others had tail and neck defects; however, despite these details, the test made it clear that the analysis was normal.

I've read that a man, to be considered fertile, needs twenty million sperm per milliliter of semen. Of those, only about two hundred courageous ones reach the fallopian tubes, and only one scores the goal.

Since each donation is different (these results, for example, were more promising than my earlier ones), the lab sent the sperm to be frozen. In case of a future donation with a lower quality, it would be possible to use any of the normal and fast sperm donated on that spring morning.

I could now hand over the ninety thousand dollars with my eyes closed. After news like that, any risk was worth it.

I then grabbed the list of previous clients and called José in Boston to ask him about the process of having his daughter, who had been born a year earlier. I needed to prepare for what was around the corner. José was the only one on the list who spoke Spanish. I also called Steve in Chicago, who had had twins, and Lane in Los Angeles, who had had a girl and a boy in 2000. None of them picked up, so I left messages. I persisted, but no one returned my calls. I tried one more time with each of them, but got only their machines. A week passed. Total silence.

In an instant, everything can be turned upside down.

Dinner was ready. A Cuban feast: white rice, black beans, ripe plantains with olive oil and cilantro, grilled chicken. In New York, with the exception of a few restaurants, it's difficult to find good Cuban food that isn't peppered with influences from other Caribbean cuisines.

Gonzalo set our long dark-wood table, and our friends Carla and the painter Cuenca argued nonstop about art and politics. Cuenca had brought two friends who happened to live on our block: Luis, a writer for the *Wall Street Journal*, and his wife, Becky, who worked for NBC.

The dinner was to celebrate a gathering with friends, but it also gave us the chance to announce that we were putting the apartment up for sale and that we were in the process of having a child.

At the table, I explained to our guests the surreal encounter with the agency, the reasons I had chosen it, and the sense of being held captive by strangers. When I told them that I would have to hand over the exorbitant figure of ninety thousand dollars in a single blow, Cuenca let out a cry and dropped his cutlery, Carla laughed, and Becky, fascinated by the story, began to talk about a friend of hers who had also started with Growing Generations for the same reasons: it was the largest and most prestigious agency. But in the end, he had settled on a smaller one in San Diego, and he was now the happy father of twins.

That's when I too dropped my cutlery. I wanted that friend's name, his phone number; I needed to talk to him right then and there.

How had I never run into someone who had been through the same thing as me before? I felt that I was in the presence of another sign.

The next day, I reached out to Becky, my guardian angel, someone who had given me a light in the labyrinth, and she helped me line up a meeting with Greg.

Greg was a single father of a two-year-old girl and boy who worked for a marketing firm in Manhattan. When he found out his children were on their way, he moved to a house in the suburbs.

"You can now see their personalities. It's amazing how different they are," he told me.

Sure enough, Greg's first choice, due to its prestige, had been Growing Generations. Like me, he went through the interviews, the office visits, and the same feeling of having a fatal disease that the agency could help us survive.

The first hurdle he'd faced was having to hand over the money in advance. The second, and the one that most influenced his decision to find another agency, was not being able to access the database of gestational mothers before signing. Finally, when he started this process, about three years earlier, the waiting list to find the ideal gestational mother was said to exceed twelve months.

I told him that none of the clients they had recommended had answered my calls. I was worried that I wouldn't find anyone who was satisfied with the process, even if they had become parents.

Greg noted that times had changed. He had heard that the agency's database of gestational mothers had grown and that the waiting list was shorter as a result. He had some friends who had worked with Growing Generations, and they were satisfied.

But in that moment, I didn't care. I immediately decided to follow in Greg's footsteps: to hire his surrogacy agency, his assisted reproductive doctor, his attorney, and his egg donation agency. Also, if possible, I wanted to hire the same gestational mother. I decided to follow a stranger, step by step, who at least was a stranger with whom I had felt some connection: Greg was the first person I'd met who'd had his children with a gestational mother.

My mind was made up. I'd go from paying for the services of a prestigious agency on luxurious Wilshire Boulevard, in the heart of Los Angeles, to trusting a small, relatively unknown agency in Chula Vista, part of greater San Diego.

Greg would be my guide.

THE PROMISED LAND

MY DAUGHTER WOULD NO longer be conceived in Oregon. Now she would be born in California. To be more precise, in San Diego. Years ago, hundreds of thousands of adventurers and desperadoes had traveled to California, the promised land, searching for gold. Now it was my turn, in search of a child.

Attorney Thomas Pinkerton, who would be our legal guide, was very clear in explaining that, of all the jurisdictions in the country, California courts were the ones that most protected the parties involved in a pregnancy that included a gestational mother, an egg donor, and the future parents.

So why had I gone to Oregon in the first place? For that matter, why had I considered Massachusetts and even New Jersey? Sometimes we drift down paths that lead nowhere. But we learn from everything. It's part of the process.

Now, I could see, physically and legally, all the parties involved. At that point, many of those faces were still unknown to me. Still, I was learning to trust strangers.

I'm going to create you, my child, with the help of two strangers. One will donate a microscopic cell and another will lend her womb to carry you for nine months. And then they will both let you go and you will belong to me—and the laws will protect me. I repeated this to myself over and over again. To make me feel (and be) safe, the lawyer recommended that I seek documentation to support that statement.

In 1993, a case filed in the California Supreme Court found that the gestational mother had no maternal rights to the baby she carried in her womb and that contracts related to gestational surrogacy were legal and enforceable. Better yet, that case highlighted that when two mothers—the gestational mother and the one who intended to have and raise the newborn—claimed custody of the baby, California law ruled in favor of the intentional mother, not the gestational one. And so, although both could prove their motherhood, the law favored the one who'd signed the contract to ensure that she had a child with a donated egg and a gestational mother.

In 1998—different case—a couple decided to have a child with a gestational mother. Neither of the prospective parents contributed their genetic code. In cases like that, the embryo is formed with a donated egg and sperm; that is, neither of them is the biological parent of the baby. And in an instant, everything changed: the future father filed for divorce just six days before the baby was due. The man claimed that, since he wasn't the biological father, he couldn't be forced to adopt the baby, that the baby didn't belong to him, that he didn't have any responsibility for a child to whom he had not contributed a single chromosome. The California Court of Appeals was drastic in its resolution: the couple—that is, both of them—had an unequivocal obligation to become the sole parents responsible for the baby.

In short, if someone conceives a baby, and presents a legal document that states that the child is the result of his or her act of creation—whether or not their own chromosomes are in play—

California law determines that that person and no one else is the baby's parent or parents.

That sounds wonderful. It's what my ears would like to hear from the judge overseeing my own case.

Of course, there's a big difference: my daughter is *mine*. She has been mine since the day I dreamed of her, and she will be mine until my last day of existence.

Since I'm going to conceive her through gestational surrogacy rather than traditional surrogacy—she will come from me and an anonymous egg donor—she will also belong to me by law. Before she's born, the gestational mother will legally abandon any intention to keep her at the time she comes into the world, so at birth I won't have to adopt her; I will already be her natural and legal father. I'll have custody, before a judge, before she sees the light of day.

So on the birth certificate, I will appear as her father, but not immediately. I'll need to overcome a series of intricate legal procedures so that the name of the woman who carried her in her womb doesn't appear in the "mother" section. Per California law, the space for the mother's name on the birth certificate cannot be left blank, so my name will go there; hence, once she is born, she'll have me, at least in the legal documents, filling both roles. Later, the lawyer will file a request to redo the birth certificate so as to identify me as the father and leave a couple of dashes in the mother's space.

There's still a long way to go before I start worrying about these little things. Now the key is to find a gestational mother who is willing to blindly throw herself into this project with me and is also willing to give me my daughter without the slightest hesitation.

I know that the law will protect me, that contracts related to surrogacy in California can be enforced, but will I be prepared for a battle if the gestational mother has a last-minute crisis and decides to raise my daughter against my will? What if her hormones kick in and a physical force greater than reason makes her close the door to her hospital room, not allowing me to even meet my daughter? Would I have the strength to go to court and drown myself in incomprehensible legal jargon, spend thousands and thousands of dollars—which I do not have—to defend, before a judge, that each cell, each organ, each part of that newborn belongs to me at a genetic level, and not to the kind woman who agreed to offer her womb to finish her development? Would I be prepared to be without my daughter for weeks, months, and maybe years, until a court ruled that she was mine—or worse, awarded us joint custody in which I could see her only every fortnight and during half of her vacation time?

What if that kind woman ultimately intended to keep her not because she loved the child, not because she considered herself her mother, but because she wanted to get child support from me, which a judge would grant her if joint custody were approved?

How could I survive such a tragedy? What precedents are there in surrogacy that support my concerns, or that could reassure me—if there is reassurance to be had in a process like this—that my daughter is going to be mine and only mine?

SURROGATE ALTERNATIVES

APRIL 2, 2004

A FRIEND WHO HAS IMMEDIATE plans to become a father told me that he's terrified by the debt that he'll have to incur: "Just thinking about the thousands of dollars it's going to cost and how far I'm going to push my credit card limits makes me shudder. I can't sleep," he says.

But the worst part about starting the search for a baby with a gestational mother is not the exorbitant prices. The most exasperating thing, what makes me shudder and lose sleep, what paralyzes me and gives me tachycardia, is the uncertainty.

You get used to a continuous sense of mistrust that you don't have time to assess. You accept it and, as if it were an incurable disease, you learn to survive with it. It's like being isolated on an island within another island. I can't stand islands, living completely surrounded by water. There's nothing you can do; your fate is sealed, like a prison sentence.

The future is murky, but at least you get to help design it so that it presents itself the way you imagine—I take comfort in that. The chance to know where we're going to procreate the embryo, who is going to manipulate the two cells that will unite so that you, my future child, can take your first steps, the first real ones, fills me with fright.

Now I imagine my daughter at a cellular level. What will be the magic egg or the valiant sperm that will contribute my chromosomes? What will I contribute? My eyes, my mouth, my nose, my height? Perhaps my curiosity, my elusive memory, my constant need to have a project in hand, my indecision, my clumsiness.

Today I think of that valiant sperm. What matters now is that I find the other genetic half to make you come true. You are progressively closer.

The Surrogate Alternatives website has an accessible database. I feel like I'm doing well, that I can navigate these waters without problems. The drop wasn't as terrible as it seemed from above.

What strikes me is that, unlike other agencies I've consulted, Surrogate Alternatives doesn't require that I pay before seeing the available gestational mothers or egg donors. Photos of an army of women emerge: age, race, and donor experience provided. It's a good sign.

Diana Van De Voort-Perez—a blond, light-eyed woman who appears to be in her forties—is the president and founder of Surrogate Alternatives. She has been an egg donor five times, all successful. In 1998 she herself was the gestational mother in a process that gave way to twins. In 2003 she lent her womb again and had a daughter. All the women who work in the agency have been donors or gestational mothers. Diana and her team know the process firsthand. It's a small agency that operates from Diana's home in Chula Vista.

I open the photos of everyone who works at the agency and scrutinize them for hours, until the individuals become familiar to me.

I check the gestational mothers page and then go to the egg

donors page. I must focus. One group at a time. The selection is too complex to allow myself the luxury of distraction. I examine these women as if they were parading before me on a beauty pageant stage.

I start with the egg donors. They all look similar to me; they all have the same smile, all hope that a photo, perhaps taken by a relative with an imprecise camera under the most inappropriate light, captures everything a future father looks for in them: beauty, intelligence, health, strength of character, humanity, bulletproof genes . . .

There I find Onaletia, one of the most experienced donors, and newcomers Lauren, Shawna, Michelle, and Danielle. None of them convinces me. Onaletia might work, but I guess— given what I read about her experience and success rate—she must be one of the most expensive donors. How much could her egg cost? We're not there yet. For now, I just anxiously check faces. Most come from California—from San Diego, to be exact. Many are students or wives of soldiers settled on the city's bases. They post photos from their childhood, some featuring siblings, and almost all share the classic high school graduation images, where they look like cardboard princesses. Most of them wear excessive makeup, which makes them look older than they really are. Their average age is twenty-four, though there are those who are too young, and some who are pushing thirty. For me, the younger the better. Nothing ages faster than a woman's egg.

Could Onaletia be an option? Gonzalo is attracted to Danielle, who looks slender, like a model, but has what strikes me as a cold expression. Since I began talking with Melinda, the agency's coordinator, reality keeps making me stumble: it turns out Danielle has already been hired by a couple and is undergoing genetic testing.

Moving on from egg donors, I review the different gestational mothers available: many of them don't work with single men, some are unwilling to abort if the fetus has issues, and most don't have health insurance that covers gestational motherhood.

Melinda recommends Mary, a gestational mother who already went through all the genetic tests and began the treatment to get pregnant for another couple, but the future parents decided to cancel the cycle.

After talking with Melinda, I go back to the Surrogate Alternatives page and find Mary. In the main photo, she's with her daughter and sister. She looks white; her daughter's skin is slightly darker, like her sister's. Her description says that her menstrual period is irregular and that she doesn't work with single men.

Melinda tells me that she will update Mary's file but that she's sure she would work with me. The irregular period isn't important, because she isn't going to be the egg donor, Melinda notes.

There's nothing else to look for. If they recommend her, what else do I need? Done: the gestational mother is going to be Mary.

I print the contract with the agency, sign it, send the questionnaire about my life—the same responses that Thorsen's Surrogate Foundation and Growing Generations received earlier—and make the first bank transfer. Melinda is going to coordinate a phone call with Mary and then a meeting with her in Chula Vista. Mary must receive my profile, read my answers to the questionnaire, rummage through my photos, and accept me. Or not. I feel like I'm taking the most expensive and exclusive college entrance exam in the country.

With the gestational mother selected—at least on my end—I tell Melinda that I'll be looking for the egg donor at A Perfect Match. If that's what Greg did, why go any other way?

I don't want to deal with more risks than those I will inevitably have to face.

We talk to Esther María, Gonzalo's sister who lives in Los Angeles, about our progress thus far, and she is moved. We tell her about the possibility of having twins or triplets. We laugh when we say that twins would be a headache, but triplets would be a nightmare. "Well, you can give me one," she says.

They will not be triplets, they just *can't* be, and even if four came out—although I would never transfer four embryos, so that possibility truly is out of the picture—they would all grow up with me.

BABY M

APRIL 5, 2004

As I was browsing the A Perfect Match donor database, I received an email: "Mary is willing to work with you. She read your questionnaire and wants to help you find your child. You will be able to talk on the phone on Saturday, and then we'll coordinate your visit so that you can meet her in person."

Gonzalo was in the kitchen. I printed Mary's photo and said, "It's her; there's no need to search any further. Mary will be the gestational mother."

He looked at me, puzzled by my sudden certainty. Knowing me, he assumed that I had gone through painstaking research to reach that conclusion.

But that's not what happened. I didn't analyze anything; I didn't dig deep to find out who she was, or go into detail about the reasons why Mary had started working with a couple and the cycle had been interrupted. It wasn't her fault—I knew that from Melinda. Her womb was ready; the couple was not. That was enough for me.

Mary had passed the agency's review process, had made it through the psychological test, and had accepted me. What more could I ask for? After losing four years, a week felt like a century to me.

I sent the photo to my mother and sister, who were delighted. "She has a very sweet face," my mother said.

With Mary by my side, I was elated, yes—but also daunted by the risk of becoming another Baby M case.

When starting the surrogacy process, you know that the chances of a positive outcome are slim, but at the same time you want to believe that you're the exception. Some obstacles are totally beyond your control: the eggs simply aren't fertilized, the embryo doesn't attach to the uterus lining, there's a miscarriage within a few weeks or even late in gestation. But there's one misfortune that you *can* impact and that you want to do everything within your power to avoid: a repeat of the Baby M case.

About 35 years ago, Mary Beth, a housewife who hadn't finished high school, married to a garbage collector, signed a contract in which she agreed to be a surrogate mother for William and Elizabeth—a biochemist and a pediatrician—so that they could have their child. For ten thousand dollars, Mary Beth agreed to lend her womb and donate an egg, meaning that the hopeful parents would be using the artificial insemination method with William's sperm. Elizabeth wasn't infertile, but the couple feared that a pregnancy could accelerate her latent multiple sclerosis.

Mary Beth and her husband had two children. He'd had a vasectomy, so it was clear that the couple didn't plan on having any more kids. In the contract, Mary Beth gave up her parental authority and any custody of the child or children she would conceive, as well as her right to contact or maintain the slightest emotional bond with them. Furthermore, she agreed to abort—if William asked her—if the fetus developed some kind of congenital anomaly. That agreement was signed in February 1985. A year and a month later, a beautiful and healthy girl, Melissa (Baby M), was born through an exhausting and painful natural childbirth, one like most deliveries. And in an instant, life changed for Mary Beth, Elizabeth, and William.

Mary Beth decided to keep the child, whom she had begun to call Sara, even though she had given her up legally long before conceiving her. When the infant was three days old, on Easter Sunday, Mary Beth did pass Baby M on to the hands of her intentional and legal parents, William and Elizabeth. However, she refused to accept her ten-thousand-dollar payment.

Despair, regret, and lack of control led Mary Beth to William and Elizabeth's house to ask them to let her have the girl for a week. They agreed. Mary Beth, who was crazy about the newborn, ran away with her and even managed to pass Baby M to her husband through a window to evade the police. They remained fugitives for three months.

At the end of a trial that lasted just over a month and garnered national attention, a New Jersey judge ruled that William and Elizabeth were the parents of Baby M, which gave validity to the surrogacy contract.

During the trial, a phone call between William, Baby M's biological and legal father, and Mary Beth, the surrogate mother, exposed the instability and anguish that tormented the latter. When the father said that he wanted his daughter back, Mary Beth lost it. "Forget it," she replied. "I'm telling you right now that I'd rather see the girl and me dead than give her to you."

Three years after signing the vilified surrogacy contract, Mary Beth and her husband obtained a ruling in their favor from the New Jersey Supreme Court, which decided that the contract had been invalid for one simple reason: in that state, no economic transaction for a woman to relinquish her rights as a mother is legal. The contract, therefore, was considered illegal.

That said, the court granted William (but not Elizabeth) custody of Baby M, adding that a judge would determine Mary Beth's visitation rights with the baby.

The ruling was a partial victory for both Mary Beth and William. However, one question remained: Over the years, what would Baby M think of it all?

Thanks in part to the publicity the case received, Mary Beth became something of a celebrity, and surrogacy came to the forefront of the country's public opinion. She claimed to have suffered public humiliation and to have been mired in pain. The only things that kept her afloat, she said, were Sara's smile—the girl remained Sara to her—and her tears every time she was snatched away at the end of their visits.

Mary Beth became an opponent of surrogacy, believing it's an issue that dates back to the Bible (Hagar, a slave, served as a surrogate mother for Abraham and Sarah) and that will continue to exist as long as poor women exist. The truth is that you pay dearly for your mistakes. And yet Mary Beth, who claimed to have breastfed the infant during the months she was on the run, and who *lived* for the time she shared with her—two hours a week, alternate weekends, and two weeks in the summer— couldn't influence Baby M's decision once she turned eighteen.

Melissa went to court and voluntarily terminated the maternal rights of her surrogate mother, Mary Beth. She also legalized the process before a judge so that Elizabeth, her intentional mother— the one who had dreamed of her, the one who had conceived her before she existed in the womb of a woman who legally gave her up—would be her one and only true mother.

A reporter talked with Melissa when the young woman was a religion major at George Washington University in Washington, DC. Melissa described herself as open to becoming a mother in the future. She told a *New Jersey Monthly* reporter:

"I love my family very much and am very happy to be with them." She was referring to William and Elizabeth, who had zealously protected her privacy since the end of the publicized case. "They're my best friends in the whole world, and that's all I have to say about it."

MARY

APRIL 7, 2004

I'VE FALLEN INTO A trap. I feel captive. I'm disoriented. I'm finally going to meet a potential gestational mother. At last I'm going to hear something real, tangible. A voice.

In some people, anxiety causes hyperactivity; it leaves me in the air, aimless. I can't read, I can't think, so I end up listening to Nina Simone.

Music isolates me. It's my therapy. I admit it: sometimes I'm the victim of my own melodrama.

At three in the afternoon in New York, twelve noon in San Diego, I'm scheduled to call Mary.

I open all the curtains in the apartment. I want New York's April light to pour in. The cold still refuses to leave the island, but the trees have already begun to blossom. I think of going for a walk in the park, around the lake, but I'd have to bundle up. I take a shower instead.

I try to imagine Mary's voice. In the photo, her smile is gentle, revealing perhaps a certain naïveté. It's one of those studio shots where a subtle filter gives the image a romantic atmosphere. Her hair is curly and full. She's a robust woman, holding her daughter on her lap, wearing a pink dress.

Nina Simone is with me until three in the afternoon.

Why am I tormenting myself? What could happen? That after saying she wants to work with me, she hears something that causes her to reject me?

Mary already knows where I was born, my age, that my parents divorced when I was two and a half, that I came to the United States when I was thirty, that I have a thick accent in English, that I have a sister and a nephew who live in Miami, that I worked as a reporter, that I now work at an entertainment magazine, that I live in New York with a partner of many years, that I don't smoke, that I don't drink. What else will she want to know?

An evaluation, a test for someone to determine, as if you were a sheep, your real value. We all need to be approved and accepted. And I know Mary is going to accept me because she read my answers—or maybe because once she too was rejected, or felt frustrated when sensing that she was being evaluated and misunderstood.

To hell with it: if she doesn't accept me, I'll find someone else. I'll find a woman who, just by hearing my voice, will know that I dreamed of you, my future child, and that I'll travel to the moon to look for you if needed. She will appear because my search has been an open book, and I'll protect that woman who decides to carry my fruit in her womb, and I'll pamper her, even if that means leaving her alone from the day you start to grow inside her.

"Mary, I lost four years searching for my child because of a doctor whose name I've already forgotten . . ."

Her voice, in response, is soft and sweet, like that of a teenage girl cautiously measuring her sentences. But what will she say about my personal melodrama?

"My mother, who is white, married my father, an Arab from Jerusalem," she tells me. "They are divorced. He now lives in

Los Angeles. I had my daughter with an African American man. I know what it's like to feel different. I won't discriminate against anyone because he's not married or because there's no mother. I know what it's like to want to be a parent and not be able to make it happen. I also know what it's like to feel rejected. So yes, I would like to help you. I'm willing to carry up to two babies, but I don't think I could do triplets."

"Mary, don't worry. I'm not planning to have triplets," I reply.

"I'm open to reduction, if that's okay with you. If we transfer three embryos and all three stick, we can do a reduction."

"Whatever you want," I answer impulsively.

Oh my God, what did I just say? Reduce a pregnancy? If all three embryos attached to Mary's uterus lining, I would have to choose which of my children I would allow to be born—that's what *reduction* means. Am I crazy? How could I tell Mary I'm going to sign a document authorizing the doctor to remove one of my babies, like in *Sophie's Choice*? But I must calm down: all three embryos aren't going to develop. That's not going to happen. I already gave Mary my word, and I did it so that she wouldn't reject me.

Mary, no: I couldn't reduce the pregnancy. I couldn't kill one of my babies, although I know they still can't think, they don't have names, they're tiny fetuses struggling to survive. But all I do is think about it, saying nothing.

She tells me about her life, her daughter, her devotion to motherhood, but I can't help picturing the needle that I might have to bury in the heart of one of my children, the weakest, the smallest one.

As impossible as it may seem, her unhurried conversation calms me down. I take notes of what she says as if I were in the middle of a job interview. I want to hang up right now and call my family to tell them who Mary is, that she was rejected once, and that she's not going to dismiss anyone for being different. I already feel like she's part of me.

Gonzalo waits in the other room, eager for an update. My sister, at work but undoubtedly thinking of me, wants to know every detail. My mom has been focused on Mary since I first mentioned her name.

Mary is twenty-three years old. She's a Capricorn. She was born in San Diego and, although her father is an Arab from Israel, she is a Christian, like her mother. When she was a teenager, she visited her paternal family in the Middle East and learned some Arabic. She lives with the father of her three-year-old daughter, an African American who works as a paramedic. She has never been married and has never had an abortion. She started working with Surrogate Alternatives in May 2003.

Mary's dream is to be a nursing assistant, and she wants to use the money she'll earn as a gestational mother—twenty thousand dollars—to "study and be able to provide a better future for my daughter." She's a healthy woman, five-foot-seven, 185 pounds, and her daughter's birth was natural. If she gets pregnant, all she asks is that they give her an epidural during the delivery. She wants to avoid, under all circumstances, a C-section, unless the doctor orders it to save the baby's life or her own.

She has never given a child up for adoption. She couldn't. That's why she is open to gestational surrogacy only.

"The baby that I will carry isn't mine; it belongs to two parents who have conceived and created it. I'm only going to allow that baby to develop," she states.

Being pregnant a few years earlier was a pleasant experience for her.

"I have a daughter, and that's enough for now. I'd like to help someone else who wants to become a parent. It's an extraordinary thing."

Both her mother and her daughter's father support her.

"My mom is going to be there for whatever I need," she assures me.

She also agrees to allow the future child, whom she will help procreate, to communicate with her in the future.

"It would be interesting to see how he or she grows up, what they become."

If the future parents—Gonzalo and I—decide an abortion is needed, she has no objection, and she's also willing to undergo amniocentesis to detect any abnormalities in the pregnancy.

Mary doesn't smoke and drinks only occasionally. As noted earlier, she lives in San Diego in a small apartment with her daughter and the father of her daughter.

Meanwhile, the bank approves my line of credit. My mother dreams that I will have a boy. My cousin Albis, who lives in Cuba, wakes up one morning and says that while she was sleeping she saw my baby: a girl.

THE SEED

APRIL 12, 2004

A PERFECT MATCH IS AN agency that offers the community a service; in that way, it's like any real estate or legal consulting agency. And, like most agencies, it places ads. In this case, in local newspapers and also at universities. The only difference is in the type of service offered: A Perfect Match offers its clients the primary genetic material to create life, eggs. The dilemma many people grapple with is whether this and similar agencies are actually selling human beings. But an egg is not a human being: an egg is a human *cell*.

In 2000, A Perfect Match caused a great stir in the assisted reproduction universe. The agency rolled out an ad in the country's most important universities requesting a donor who, if she met the future parents' required parameters, would receive a fifty-thousand-dollar compensation—until then, the highest amount ever offered for an egg.

Although an inexperienced donor (with no track record of success) can charge around three thousand dollars, those who have donated more than once, successfully, and have specific characteristics—Ashkenazi or Sephardic Jews, Hindus, or Asians, for example—can raise the figure up to twenty thousand dollars. But fifty thousand dollars seemed excessive—even more so given that the American Society for Reproductive Medicine had stipulated that a compensation of more than ten thousand dollars for donating eggs was inappropriate. What were the owners of A Perfect Match—Darlene, a former real estate agent, and her husband, Thomas Pinkerton, a renowned assisted reproduction attorney whose help I mentioned earlier—hoping to accomplish with that type of ad? Some thought publicity, but the Pinkertons said that they only wanted to help expectant parents find specific characteristics in a donor.

The Pinkertons created their agency after experiencing surrogacy firsthand. In 1990, an embryo created in a lab with both of their genetic material was transferred to the uterus of a gestational mother, who in that case was one of Thomas's aunts. When their daughter was born, the Pinkertons had to fight in court to get Darlene to appear on the birth certificate as the mother. Since then, both have dedicated themselves to helping dozens of infertile couples trying to have a family.

As I noted earlier, A Perfect Match was the same agency Greg had used, which is why—with Mary on the team—I now sign up to work with them. Unlike at Surrogate Alternatives, with A Perfect Match I have to commit and send a bank transfer before being given access to the password-protected database.

I complete the necessary requirements and Gonzalo and I begin to study the donors, some of whom we also saw advertised on the Surrogate Alternatives website. Caroline, twenty-three, of Irish descent, is in college studying biology. Laura, twenty-one, is of Italian descent, and fourteen eggs were obtained from her previous donation. Donna, twenty-four, is Catholic with light eyes. She's a mother, and twenty-one eggs were obtained from her earlier donation. Rachel, twenty-two, of Dutch descent, studies anthropology in college, but she's never been a donor. And Julieta, a twenty-one-year-old Italian, has two children and has been a donor before.

I want someone *safe*. I haven't felt a connection with any of these women that would justify choosing one. It could be any of them. We'll have to see how much money they request. Becca, our primary contact at the agency, assures me that the figures are always negotiable.

Apparently, this isn't going to be as easy as choosing Mary. In a gestational mother, we were looking for a determined and brave woman willing to carry our future child in her womb for nine months. If she was healthy, met the agency's requirements, and wanted to work with us, that was enough.

The woman who will contribute half of your genetic code, my daughter, requires a more rigorous selection process. This must be carefully thought out: a photo, a telephone conversation, college notes—none of that will define the choice.

It's true that she too will have to accept me, but I may need the agency's help now. With such a large database, the decision is difficult.

Gonzalo stops at Alicia, a twenty-two-year-old. She's a college student and has never been an egg donor. That's not a problem. At some point all experienced donors were first-timers.

I move forward in search of the seed.

I'm still waiting for a sign.

ALICIA

APRIL 14, 2004

I AM ENTHRALLED. ALICIA HAS shiny, dark, shoulder-length hair and deep-blue eyes. Her makeup is subtle. She's short and looks fragile. There are photos of her with her grandmother, her brother, and her parents.

Alicia is twenty-two years old, wears glasses, and studies political science in California. She wants to be a donor to help a couple have children. She'd like someone to help her in a similar situation. She drinks once a week—they almost all say the same thing—doesn't do drugs, has never gotten a tattoo, and has never received a blood transfusion.

She describes herself as independent, strong, perceptive, intelligent, adaptable, frugal, and having an excellent eye for detail. She has a talent for the arts and also speaks French.

Alicia would love to meet the child whom she helps procreate, but under no circumstances would she consider herself his or her mother; she'd just like to convey to the child how happy she was to help conceive him or her.

Her paternal grandmother is Spanish, Galician. And that's when she wins me over: my grandmother, also Galician, was

from Vigo. Her grandmother, she says, was elegant, sophisticated, intelligent. Her family on her mother's side is Irish.

As a child, her parents say that instead of crying, she sang.
Alicia adds that, as an adult, she really enjoys life and being
alive. She's too pragmatic to let a small thing ruin everything.

She had her first period at ten. To this day, they're regular
and last four to five days. She doesn't take birth control pills. No
one in her family has fertility issues. As a teenager, she says, her
acne was light.

Alicia is a true believer in organ donation. She sees donating an egg as similar to donating an organ to someone in need.
The financial and emotional expenses incurred by a family that
cannot conceive naturally are enormous, so donating an egg is
nothing to her.

Her parents can't afford their children's education, so she will
use the financial compensation to continue her studies in Paris.

Alicia dreams of traveling and one day settling down and
having a family. She's passionate about extending the rights of
marriage to all people. She has many gay friends who suffer
from not having the same rights. She feels, on a personal level,
very offended by homophobia, racism, anti-Semitism, and any
form of discrimination. She studies more than twelve hours a
day, volunteers at a homeless shelter, and on the weekends tries
to get as much sleep as possible. At night, she enjoys dressing up
and hanging out with her group of friends.

She considers herself a strong woman and has survived some
painful trials.

Alicia sounds like the one. Where has she been? Did I really
have to wait all these years for her to show up? Now I'm sure that
those four years, which I thought I'd lost, were in fact necessary
for Alicia to reach the minimum age required to become an egg
donor and cross my path.

MATER CERTA–PATER INCERTUS

APRIL 15, 2004

ALICIA ACCEPTS MY OFFER. Now I just have to meet Mary in person. I can't believe that my life is going to change in a matter of months. It takes only a moment, I know.

I plan to travel to San Diego. The flight from New York will stop in Los Angeles and I'll have to take a small plane from there. The Reproductive Sciences Center, the assisted reproduction clinic run by Dr. Samuel Wood, is in La Jolla. A Perfect Match, the egg donation agency, and attorney Thomas Pinkerton are in La Mesa. And the agency that provides gestational mothers, Surrogate Alternatives, is in Chula Vista. It's going to be another long journey.

First, I'll meet Diana, the founder of Surrogate Alternatives. Mary, the future gestational mother, will be waiting for me there. Then I'll go to my doctor's appointment at the reproductive clinic. A new phase of the process has begun.

Gonzalo beleaguers me with questions. What will Mary be like? Is she a good mom? How do you know she won't disappear when she gets pregnant? She's not the biological mom, but she might grow fond of the child. During nine months, she'll be nourishing the baby, singing to it at night, feeling its kicks;

she will know if it has hiccups, she will worry when it doesn't move. That baby will change her body—her breasts will swell, her mood will swing. She'll feel heavy, tired. And all for a baby whom she'll have to hand over at birth because of some papers she will have signed.

What stops her from being the mother, if she carries it for nine months in her womb?

Doesn't providing only her egg, a simple cell, exclude her, eliminate the possibility of considering herself a progenitor? I counter.

Gonzalo's doubts ramp up further. "Then what will that make me? I'll also be its father, even though I won't be contributing any chromosomes. Does that exclude me too? Me, the person who will be dedicating body and soul to that baby—what will *I* end up being?"

According to *Merriam-Webster's Collegiate Dictionary*, "father" comes from Middle English *fader*, from Old English *fæder*, and is akin to Old High German *fater* and Latin *pater*. The definition given is "a male parent; a man who has begotten a child; a male animal who has sired an offspring; *capitalized*: God; the first person of the Trinity; one that originates or institutes; a priest of the regular clergy . . ."

And mother, what is being a mother today? "Mother": two syllables, six letters, one word, several meanings. That word comes from Middle English *moder*, from Old English *mōdor*, akin to Old High German *muoter* and Latin *mater*. "A woman who has given birth to a child; a female parent; a woman in authority, specifically, the superior of a religious community of women; an elderly woman; one that has produced or nurtured something; *obsolete*: womb; feeling (as tenderness or affection) inherited from or characteristic of a mother; matrix; a particularly large, formidable, or extreme example . . ."

Mater semper certa est. This is what Roman law's classic principle states: "The mother is always known." Furthermore, *Mater est quam gestatio demonstrat*: "The mother is proven by gestation." In old Latin aphorisms, fathers fare badly. *Mater certa—pater incertus*: "The mother is known; the father, who knows?"

But nowadays, who is considered a mother? The one who gives birth to a baby, the one who provides her genetic code, or the one who intends to have the baby and raise it? There are birth mothers, genetic mothers, and intentional mothers. Fathers fall into only two categories: biological and intentional. By law, the relationship between mother and child is immediate and easy to demonstrate. The one that exists between father and child is mediate and indirect.

So what does "child" mean? "An unborn or recently born human being; a son or a daughter; an adopted child; a member of the tribe or clan; one who has been strongly conditioned by a place, a type of action or occupation, or a state of affairs; dependent, subsidiary."

From the birth of the first test-tube baby, those concepts should have been expanded. Why does the dictionary not mention that a mother or father is also the one who *intends* to be such a figure, the one who raises the baby, the one who is responsible for a child whom he or she has taken care of from the moment it was born, from the moment it was dreamed of? Why doesn't the dictionary add that a child is also the fruit of an embryo created in a lab and grown in the womb of someone who is not its gestational mother?

You, our future child, will be our daughter and we will be your parents, no matter what the dictionary says. You are and will always be our daughter.

THE EMBRACE

APRIL 16, 2004

I BOARD THE PLANE AND once again begin to write my fate's script, but I leave negative thoughts behind. I avoid pondering possible calamities so as to exclude them from my immediate future.

I'm meeting Mary that afternoon at the Surrogate Alternatives headquarters in Chula Vista. This means I have to rent a car, drive south on the San Diego freeways, and then drive north again to meet Dr. Wood at the La Jolla clinic the next morning.

Driving isn't something I enjoy, and even less so in cities I don't know. I have my favorite travel shirt ready. My blue shirt, which always looks impeccable—it must have more polyester than cotton. I want to make a good impression.

San Diego is like any other city in one way, full of highways. From the plane I can see the port. The sea's proximity calms me.

Chula Vista is south of San Diego proper. Like almost every city in the area, it has a large number of Hispanics. I read somewhere that it's the most boring city in America. I suppose that's an exaggeration.

In any case, I'm not looking for fun. As I head south, I don't feel like I'm in a city but rather a suburb, like those that predominate in Miami. A kind of Kendall, with less vegetation. Everything is brown, even the air. The houses are the color of dust. One street is the same as the next, the same as the one that follows, and I imagine the same as the one that will come later. It's a maze, but an open maze. It's easy to get lost in the confusion of colorless houses. The streets have names in Spanish—it's California, after all. I'm looking for Fifth Avenue, my destination.

I arrive at a two-story house in the middle of a neighborhood block and park. It's three in the afternoon, hot, and no one's on the street. Apparently, Diana runs her agency from her own home. There's no sign that says Surrogate Alternatives, but the number is right. Did I make a mistake when jotting down the address? I call Melinda and she confirms that yes, I'm at the right place, but they're still waiting for Mary. Perfect. I prefer getting there first, overcoming the commotion of the search, so as to relax, acclimate.

Still in the car, I think about our upcoming meeting. When Mary arrives, should I give her a kiss, a hug, my hand? Will she bring her daughter—and if so, how should I greet *her*? Did Mary go to the hairdresser in preparation, or stop indecisively in front of her closet, not knowing what to wear for this occasion? (Not the pink dress, she must've thought, because it's the same one in the agency's photo of her.) What earrings will she be wearing? Flashy? Simple? Or did she not put any on? And her nails? Nails should be neat, maybe light in color. The shoes, flat. She's tall; she doesn't need heels. The key is for her to feel comfortable so that she can also feel safe.

Melinda, who smiles in welcome, is a Californian in her forties. She's a gestational mother too.

"If I were available, I would've liked to work with you," she tells me, with an air of superiority.

No doubt about it: I'm in a *house*. Yes, with a typical wood-trimmed living room set, the kind you can purchase in a mall. The walls of the ground floor, the living room, and the dining room are painted peach. Upstairs are the offices, I guess. At the dining room table there's a woman who turns to look at me and then, without saying hello, is once again absorbed in the papers in front of her.

"She wants to be a surrogate mother," Melinda reveals. "We're going to start evaluating her."

Will they look at her uterus, the size of her breasts, her hips? Or is Melinda referring to her psychological profile, to her ability to carry a child in her womb for nine months and then let it go? Has someone told that potential donor that, even if she carries the baby in her womb for nine months, it won't be hers; it won't resemble her or anyone in her family?

We go upstairs and Melinda introduces me to Diana, who is on the phone. Diana is beautiful, short, and her body shows no sign that it went through several deliveries, one of them twins, or donated eggs five times. Diana apologizes and continues her call.

Leading me to a different office, Melinda explains that the idea of this meeting is for Mary and me to spend a few minutes alone—as long as we need. We should ask each other questions and address any concerns we may have. We should convince each other—or not—that we're taking the right step, because once the embryos are transferred to her womb, attach themselves to her uterus lining, and the pregnancy is carried to term, there will be no turning back.

Glancing through the window, I see a woman approaching. "That's Mary," Melinda tells me. I have such palpitations that I think Mary is going to notice them through my wrinkle-free blue shirt.

Mary did *not* go to the salon, I see. Her hair is pulled up casually. She didn't put on makeup or do her nails. Her eyes are subtly lined, as if retaining a trace from the night before. She's wearing a white T-shirt, faded jeans, sandals, and no earrings.

She looks very young. She's tall and robust, but her girlish voice and appearance make her seem fragile. Melinda points us toward the main sofa and hands us an album with agency photos before leaving us alone.

One of the photos shows a group of women posing with smiles. Mary tells me that those are her peers in the counseling sessions that surrogates must attend every month once they start working with expectant parents.

"I don't like them that much," she reveals. Her voice, at that moment, is lower than usual. "They're older, and I'm not very talkative."

I feel as if she's subtly trying to indicate that I shouldn't expect much from her. That she's rather reserved. The album is full of pregnant women with huge bellies covered in stretch marks.

Going for full disclosure, she adds, "Remember what I said on the phone? One is fine, I'd even be willing to try two, but . . . with three you'd have to be open to reduction." She softens her reminder with a shy smile.

Continuing through the photo album, I recognize Greg. There he is with his twins, in the delivery room, along with Suham, the gestational mother, who's Hispanic and speaks Spanish. She would have been perfect for me, but she isn't available. Working with Suham would have meant following Greg in every way, my initial goal; but something tells me that Mary will be the perfect gestational mother. A woman who doesn't talk much, won't require a great deal of time, will take care of my child, will eat healthy food, will give birth without complications, will speak softly to the baby, and will hand him or her over with a smile.

I imagine *myself* in the photo album, excited about my baby as

Mary happily hands her to me. Someone in the future will look at our photo and imagine themselves in the following year's album. In their case, perhaps with twins, or even triplets, because the gestational mother won't have qualms about carrying them in her womb and would never demand a reduction, as Mary has done. I understand her reservations on that front, even though I have a few of my own.

Mary doesn't have much time today because her daughter is waiting for her at school. After half an hour of conversation, she rises and tells me I can call her anytime. That everything will be fine. That she's happy to be working with me. That I'm going to become a dad soon.

I hug her, grateful. Our embrace lasts only a few seconds, but in that gesture we make a pact. In that instant, we are united.

THE CLINIC

APRIL 19, 2004

I T's 9:30 A.M., AND in half an hour I'll be visiting the lab where we're going to conceive my daughter. I'm not in a science center, with immaculate walls and gleaming glass. I'm in a mall, with a brick facade and a pizzeria, a coffee shop, and a real estate office on the ground floor. The Reproductive Sciences Center is on the second floor, a maze of gray offices and hallways. I get lost. I search for the office number but wind up at the elevator again. I call and Suham, the receptionist, also the gestational mother of Greg's children, gives me the coordinates.

On the door leading into the center, I read a warning: "Before crossing the threshold and entering the room, avoid wearing any type of perfume." Oh God, I think I might have perfume on my jacket. I sniff for the slightest trace, but my senses are dulled. I smell nothing. I can't distinguish anything beyond the building's prevailing scent. My sense of smell has never been among my best attributes.

The waiting room is small, quiet, and sparsely populated. Suham greets me warmly and has me take a seat. Within a few minutes I'm called to the front and she introduces me to Angela, who is in charge of processing the documentation. *Lots* of documentation.

Then more blood tests. The doctor wants to eliminate the possibility of any type of congenital disease, or at least know what to expect. I must sign an order for the frozen sperm sample in the LA lab to be transferred to La Jolla for testing. Again? Wasn't the analysis that assured me I could have a child enough? What else do they want to look for? Should I worry?

Dr. Linda Anderson, the center's embryologist and andrologist (male reproductive specialist), says, "Now we have to analyze your sperm with precision, to move forward safely."

I explain that four years ago I abandoned the idea of having a child because an analysis had not turned out as expected—or rather, because it had been read arbitrarily. Later, I was assured at Growing Generations that I was fertile, that my sperm results wouldn't be a problem with IVF.

"I want you to get an SCSA," says Dr. Anderson. Another acronym that I'll have to memorize. This is a state-of-the-art study called the sperm chromatin structure assay, which goes beyond a simple sperm analysis—itself already fairly complex. The SCSA measures the quality of DNA, or genetic material, evaluating the twenty-three chromosomes that reside in the sperm's head, made up of chromatin, which consist of DNA and proteins. The study was first put into practice around 1980, and in the years since, it's been confirmed as a very useful technique to determine the quality of semen.

The assay, or test, consists of taking a sample of five thousand sperm, which are scanned to analyze their chromosomes' level of damage or fragmentation. If the result is greater than 30 percent, a man's fertility level is considered poor or deficient. The technique also measures the frozen sperm's DNA susceptibility when it is handled with certain types of acids.

It's not that sperm with fragmented DNA can't fertilize an egg, Dr. Anderson explains. A damaged sperm *can* produce a living embryo, but in the end that embryo, which may even implant itself and grow in the uterus, won't reach the pregnancy's full term. The SCSA minimizes the chances of that happening: even certain semen samples that have been considered acceptable in terms of motility, quality, and morphology by earlier testing may be assessed as abnormal in an SCSA test.

As a man ages, the level of fragmentation of his chromosomes increases and, as a result, his fertility decreases. In other words, the biological clock doesn't affect just women; men also experience a decline in their ability to procreate. One of the factors that causes DNA fragmentation has to do with the environment and exposure to chemicals, pesticides, and herbicides.

The clinic will be sending my frozen sample to South Dakota for the SCSA, Dr. Anderson says. She also recommends that I get tested for the presence of antisperm antibodies.

After I assimilate that deluge of information, she adds with a comforting smile, "It's the only way to be sure."

But I know that certainty doesn't exist. Intentional fathers throw a cell into the air to see what happens. We're in the hands of the unknown, of strangers. Yes, I will undergo all the tests. If they want, they can send my entire body to South Dakota, take samples of my skin, of my brain. I just want to finish the tests and spring into action.

Next up: Dr. Samuel Wood. He's wearing a scrub top. There are pictures of babies in his office—most of whom, I suppose, he helped procreate. He leans back in his banker's chair, puts both hands behind his neck, and sighs, relaxed.

"With a gestational mother and an egg donor, your chances of having a child are greater than if you tried to expand your family only with a surrogate mother," he says.

Dr. Wood has the gift of reassurance.

"What about the tests you now have to do on one of my most precious fluids?" I ask him, a little distraught.

"Let's wait for the results. You've already come very far."

I tell him about Mary, the good connection we made; about my fascination with Alicia, the beautiful egg donor, who has shiny dark hair and deep-blue eyes. I'm sure he must be used to dealing with somewhat passionate patients. Who knows where I fall in this range? Maybe I'm too hopeful. But why should I be negative?

"We have a high rate of babies born to egg donors and surrogate mothers. We trust our team, and what we do. We will transfer the best embryos; the rest we will preserve in case we need to try again," he explains.

I imagine an army of embryos waiting to be transferred, stored for decades in sophisticated tanks. Hundreds of thousands of future human beings, of all races, ready for the battle of life. And at the same time, I realize—or rather, react to—the reality that he's presenting: nothing is 100 percent certain. There's a high risk that the embryo transfer won't work, that the uterus won't be fully prepared.

"The uterus lining must reach the right thickness; then the quality of the embryo comes into play," Dr. Wood tells me. "We assign embryos different categories, depending on their morphology and cell division. We can implant several class A embryos—strong contenders—but not all of them will develop. For an embryo to become a human being, that's in the hands of God."

I want the conversation to continue, I want him to further explain the process, but I imagine there must be a surrogate mother waiting for him, ready to receive a catheter with robust embryos. I feel like I'm in a science fiction scene, maybe at an engineering center where everything is possible. His job is "to facilitate man's basic instinct," says the doctor, and pauses. Too long a pause for me. What is that instinct?

"The desire to have a child," he concludes. "I'm sure that you, even as a youngster, visualized your future. You probably saw yourself as a parent. Many young people do. Some may never include a child in their future, but for most, a life without children feels incomplete."

Many of the patients who come to his practice begging for help are couples who, now in their forties, have achieved everything they set out to do: a great and stable job, a substantial bank account, the home and cars of their dreams. Now they need only a child. But they start trying for it, and it doesn't come. The eggs have aged, or some other problem exists. What can they do then? Assisted reproduction.

"Our clinic is small," Dr. Wood says. "We don't accept more cases than we can handle."

As he continues to explain the road ahead, a phrase he used earlier—one that I've unsuccessfully tried to ignore—echoes in my mind: "in the hands of God." I find it hard to believe that this man, a scientist who manipulates cells until they turn into embryos, leaves it to God for those cells, which soon multiply toward infinity, to become a baby.

"We prepare surrogate mothers and egg donors, observe fertilization, transfer the embryos, and follow the pregnancy every two weeks until the end of the first trimester. At twelve weeks, the gestational mother is referred to an obstetrician, as in any other normal pregnancy."

That means I have three months of agony ahead of me, before Mary—assuming our first effort "takes"—is referred to the doctor who will treat her until she's ready to deliver. In reality, of course, my anxiety will not cease until I have my beautiful baby in my arms, until I see him or her on a plane with me and we leave Los Angeles to go home.

Submerged in terrible uncertainty, at least I have the satisfaction of being one step further along. The bank has approved my line of credit, the players have been chosen, the final sperm tests have been initiated—so let's get on with it!

Now the waiting begins. Every day is a week, every week is a month, every month is a year.

THE PIONEER

I COULD NEVER GIVE MY own child up," says Mary. "I'm not ready for traditional surrogacy, because if it were my egg, it would be my child, and I wouldn't be able to hand him or her over. What we're going to do is different. I'll be carrying your child, not mine. It's clear in my mind that from the moment that baby is born, it will belong to you."

The more I listen to her, the more convinced I am that Mary is ready. She has never given a child up for adoption, as I already knew, and wouldn't consider going through artificial insemination for financial gain. She even assures me that she doesn't feel capable of donating her eggs.

"They would always be my biological children," she explains.

I understand her. I'm on her side. I couldn't give up a child either. Donating an egg is like donating any vital organ. That a father or a mother or two parents are the ones who *intend* to be parents—those who will raise the child conceived through traditional surrogacy—doesn't exclude the sense of disorientation and abandonment that could come from seeing a baby leave in someone else's arms. I try to understand the mindset of traditional surrogate mothers and the emotional—and legal—conflicts that could arise.

As proof of this, there's Elizabeth Kane, who's the first publicly acknowledged woman to sign a legal contract to become a surrogate mother in the United States and receive monetary compensation. She gave birth to beautiful baby Justin in 1980 and gave him to the intentional parents, despite having provided half of the baby's chromosomes. The other half belonged to the father, a stranger to her.

Elizabeth Kane, which was the pseudonym she used to sign the contract, became a celebrity when news of the arrangement got out. She had her fifteen minutes of fame, and to this day has been unable to recover. Giving that baby up was far harder than she'd imagined. During the grueling battle that later put the country's concept of surrogacy at risk with the Baby M case, Elizabeth served as an adviser to Mary Beth, the remorseful surrogate mother from New Jersey. The irony is that Elizabeth's real name is Mary Beth.

That woman, who had become a surrogate mother to help an infertile couple despite her husband's opposition, was now one of the creators of the National Coalition Against Surrogacy, for which she even testified before Congress.

Her book, *Birth Mother*, is a plea against a practice she pioneered. A trap of fate. When she accepted by legal contract that the baby she would birth wouldn't belong to her, that cutting the umbilical cord would end any kind of physical connection with it, she never imagined the maelstrom in which she would find herself once the child was born. The judicial system could snatch the child from her arms, she said, but not from her memory. As she saw it, she was condemned for life to drown in her own guilt. Her therapy, I guess, was fighting against what she herself helped establish.

Elizabeth, thirty-seven, was married with three children.

Some members of her family suffered from infertility, and it was frustrating for her to see their devastation. A small ad in the local newspaper requesting a surrogate mother caught her eye. It was from a Louisville couple who couldn't have children. She managed to convince her husband, who was reluctant to support her participation, and finally contacted them.

When she was three months pregnant, Elizabeth became a public figure. Although she didn't want to be called by her real name or have her town or state identified, she agreed to pose for *People* magazine with her three children. "I'm very grateful for what I do," she told the magazine. Meanwhile, her husband was convinced that her decision would end up dividing their family. Elizabeth didn't like the idea of accepting money to be a surrogate mother. Her husband even mentioned that they didn't need the money. "I'd do it for free," Elizabeth said at one point. However, she accepted the ten thousand dollars to carry the intentional parents' baby in two payments: the first one when the pregnancy was confirmed, and the second when the adoption documents were finalized.

She made it clear to *People* magazine that when the baby was born, it would belong to the father. "I'm simply growing it for him." She knew that this child wouldn't return home with her, that there would be no family arguments about what to name him, as had happened when she had her son. Furthermore, she realized that she didn't actually want a new member in her family. Their finances wouldn't allow it. However, she claimed that she loved him from the moment he was conceived and that she spoke to him softly every time he moved or kicked her belly.

The one who suffered the most during the process was her son. When it became public that Elizabeth had accepted thousands of dollars, the kids at school mocked him, making fun of how much a baby cost.

It seemed simple and well-orchestrated at the time: she gave the child to the father, who thanked her for helping to complete their family. The man's gratitude moved her, and she was satisfied, knowing that she had carried the baby as a gift of love. David, her husband, never stopped thinking that this baby could ruin their lives. And he was right.

Eight years later, in *Birth Mother*, Elizabeth talked about how the entire process of getting pregnant and the mistrust of those around her plunged her into a terrible state of disarray. When Justin was born, she wrote him a goodbye letter that included the words: "You don't belong to me."

She thought that would be enough, but life began to get complicated after the birth. Her relationship with her husband changed, and her legal and genetic son fell into a practically chronic depression. He suffered the loss of a brother he'd never actually had. He felt as if his mother had given birth to a stillborn baby. A child lost in limbo, a baby he most likely considered his brother.

As it turns out, Elizabeth bore a guilt that had begun in 1966. At twenty-two years old and unmarried, she became pregnant, had a girl, and immediately put her up for adoption. She never recovered from that loss. Neither her marriage nor her three children had made her forget about the girl she'd abandoned. Maybe that's why she decided to become a surrogate mother. Perhaps she thought that might heal her wounds, but the damage wound up being greater because, in the end, it not only destroyed her life but also severed her innocent family.

ALL THE INFORMATION I've studied about surrogate mothers has made me feel even more confident about not choosing the traditional surrogacy path. At least Mary is aware that the baby she will carry in her womb won't have the slightest genetic connection to her. Yes, it's true, she will receive financial compensation, as did Elizabeth, but even all the money in the world couldn't pay for what Mary is going to do for me. She's going to provide her body to host a life that doesn't belong to her; she's going to participate in a true act of human creation. Her satisfaction is based on making others happy, without having to abandon her own child. That's her essence. The only one that can prevail in a gestational mother. It's crystal-clear to her. And to me, that's a miracle.

THE PRESENCE OF GOD

APRIL 22, 2004

From each stage of life, even those most distant in time, we remember at least one scene. It can be a feeling, a place, a state of mind. It almost always involves an anecdote. Old photographs help us remember, as do family stories and the indelible impact of deaths, births, major political events, and wars.

I have etched in my memory the day I couldn't walk. I can still see myself in the dark room—the sole window facing an inner courtyard—of Tía Romelia's gas-smelling apartment, a bowl of chicken soup before me for my fever. My three cousins jumped on the bed in the adjacent room, and I was unable to join them because my legs were failing me. My aunt had a rosary and had made a promise to God—I can't remember what it was—if he granted me the power to walk again. I was three years old. I also remember that my father carried me on his shoulders to the Children's Orthopedic Hospital in Havana. It was early in the morning, and cold—it's rarely cold in Cuba. To think of how much can be etched in the memory of a three-year-old terrifies me.

To this day, I'm not sure whether my legs were paralyzed from a high fever or because of the spinal deviation with which

I was born. What I do know is that my paralysis was never discussed as I grew older. No one ever mentioned it again. But it was recorded in my mind.

Or was it? Once, I asked my aunt if she knew why I had been paralyzed when I was three years old, and she claimed not to have the slightest recollection of the event; yet she's one of those people who keep the first tooth that you lost or the little pebble that got stuck in your nose one summer and had to be removed in the emergency room. I then checked with my mom, who said it never happened—but she hadn't been there: she was on her way to pick me up and take me back with my sister and grandmother.

When I brought my dad from Cuba to New York to meet Emma, I asked him about my paralysis. His response was blunt, with the conviction of someone who doesn't tend to mix up dates.

"I never took you to the doctor," he said. "When you were three years old, I lived out east, and I'm sure I didn't go to Havana that day."

The irony is that I can still recall in great detail a scene from when I was three years old, that perhaps never even happened, but I'm vague on certain more recent details. My memory suffered an apparent gap between September 2000 and January 2004. The two sperm tests are the limits of that parenthesis. In those four years, devastating events happened on a personal and professional level, and even the city where I live had the worst year in its history. But in my memory, during those four years I see myself alone, in an abyss, with my heart on the verge of giving up. My memory is imprecise—as I've said before, I tend to push adverse moments into oblivion—but, when reviewing old emails recently, I realized that I never stopped searching for you, my child, despite that abyss. There are multiple letters to various surrogacy agencies from that time. I even found one I'd sent to Surrogate Alternatives in January 2003, with Melinda's response—yet it wasn't until roughly a year later that I started the process with them.

From that dark period, I remember only one feeling: my closeness to God. Although I come from a Catholic family—my grandparents, of Spanish origin, brought their Christian tradition with them—in Cuba it was illegal to believe in God. In a college philosophy class, a Soviet professor—a graduate of Lomonosov University in Moscow—said something that left us all puzzled, not so much by the value of the idea itself, but because she dared to mention it in a state educational institution.

"God is abstract," she began. "We grew up without him. *You've* grown up without the presence of God. I've participated in studies where it's been proven that the most atheist of atheists, the man or woman most convinced that God doesn't exist, only needs to break down, face a momentous occasion—be the victim of a shipwreck, or travel on a plane that's about to crash—for God to appear as the last resort in their mind. If we're about to lose a child to an illness and the doctors no longer know what to do to save him or her, the only thing we have within our reach, or what we tend to seek as redemption, is our faith in God."

No one said a word. The professor waved her scented-cedar fan and contemplated our astonished faces, while the translator conveyed her ideas.

Did I turn to God during my dark years as the only alternative to becoming a father?

Did I take refuge in a faith that doesn't belong to me solely to save myself—or rather, to save my daughter?

My encounters with Father Alexis at the beautiful Church of the Blessed Sacrament on the Upper West Side became more and more frequent. I began to study the Bible. I found consolation in Sunday mass, and during the week I prayed and thought about my daughter. Without mentioning it to Father Alexis, I asked God for help to meet my daughter. I knew already that doctors can manipulate an egg and a sperm and cause fertilization, but I hadn't yet heard that "for an embryo to become a human being, that's in the hands of God"—and yet it was to God that I turned.

Now, having recently heard those words from Dr. Wood, I promise myself that I will open the spiritual doors for my daughter to have her own encounter with God. I will let her take refuge in a religion that she chooses herself, not in one that others might try to impose on her. I want her to have the opportunity to grow up with a faith that speaks to her, whatever that faith may be.

Growing up with the absence of God, as I did—being afraid to believe in God or enter a temple or a church—is something that I don't want to leave as an inheritance. At least that much is clear to me.

THE APPROVAL

MAY 2004

As I walk down Ninth Avenue, I get a call from someone who identifies himself as José. Who's José? I can't remember; my memory is a mess. I'm polite, I greet him, and he begins to talk to me nonstop, explaining that he received my call but wasn't able to call back right away. He was traveling, he explains. His life has been very complicated this last year. He laughs, with a certain complicity. And he speaks softly, as if he were telling me a secret.

Who *is* he?

Since the girl was born, he says, he leaves work and is with her all the time; he doesn't have time even to breathe. He no longer knows what it's like to read a book. "My experience with Growing Generations was good," he adds. I realize that it's José from Boston, one of the more than ten names that the agency had given me to receive recommendations and experiences. The only one who has answered my call. Maybe no one else answered because my voice sounded desperate, or because they didn't want to give me false hope. Because what I'm getting myself into is very, very hard.

"We have several friends who are now going through the

process with that same agency," says José. "They do a good job. The problem is that after the gestational mother gets pregnant, they forget about you."

Your call is a little late, José. I've already started the process with Surrogate Alternatives. Still, I want to hear more.

José's girl is now one. The whole process with the donor was very stressful. She was from New York; the gestational mother, from Massachusetts. Distance was an issue. In the end, the embryos didn't turn out to be of very good quality.

"If we decide to do it again," he says, apparently convinced that he will be looking for a sibling for his daughter, "I'll choose a much younger donor."

The one he used was twenty-six years old. Thank God Alicia is only twenty-two.

He says that, given the panorama presented by the embryologists, they decided that the best choice was to transfer four embryos. Luckily for him, one implanted itself.

I say goodbye to José, convinced that I've made the right decision, that I've traced the path I want. Regardless of and despite all the obstacles, I think: he got his baby girl in the end.

THE SCSA TEST came back normal," Dr. Anderson, the embryologist, tells me.

But how normal? Does that mean my sperm will work even better than I expected?

"Your score of twenty puts you in a good place, in the potential category of good fertility. We've had many successful in vitro pregnancies with numbers similar to yours," she says, filling me with hope.

However, I have other doubts, and I ask her about the morphology of my sperm. She reports a score of 9 percent, reflecting the quantity of abnormally shaped sperm.

"Nine percent isn't that terrible," she reassures me. "Many men become parents spontaneously with that same percentage, and here we achieve a good level of fertilization with that morphology. On the day of the oocyte donation, we place eggs next to sperm and hope that fertilization will be natural. We give another group of eggs an ICSI—that's an intracytoplasmic sperm injection—which means that we inject a sperm cell into an egg to fertilize it. When the eggs are obtained, we'll apply *both* techniques, depending on how your sample looks that day."

It doesn't help that Dr. Anderson tells me all the possibilities I have, that my semen looks fine and my results are normal, because the idea that I have amorphous sperm remains stuck in my mind. I imagine deformed sperm cells navigating pointlessly, unable to pierce the zona pellucida of the oocyte.

"It's very common for the morphology of some sperm to be abnormal." Apparently, Dr. Anderson has an answer for everything. "Sperm is produced in very large numbers: we're talking in the millions. It's normal for many of them to have an imperfect figure. That's what 'amorphous' means; the term doesn't have a particular clinical meaning. I don't consider your sample difficult to work with, and there's no reason to expect bad results. Of course, the sperm could have a functional defect impossible to detect with the tests that exist today . . ."

"So I *do* have to worry. There's a possibility of another undetectable imperfection."

"But it would be rare."

What a relief. Now I can breathe.

"In the meantime, you know what you can do?"

Yes, I know: Avoid Jacuzzis—they don't exist for me, nor will they exist from now on—or anything that increases my body temperature. Don't ride bicycles or smoke. Avoid any type of medicine without first consulting Dr. Wood.

The next step will be for the psychologist Sylvia Marnella,

hired by Surrogate Alternatives, to evaluate me. *Another* test—this one to determine if I'm capable of putting up with a gestational mother, a stranger, carrying you in her womb; if I'm ready to be a father; if I'm going to lose it and start chasing after the army of strangers who will be helping me find you. More questions to answer, but I've gotten used to my life being an open book. I speak once more about my childhood, my divorced parents, my departure from Cuba. Every time I tell my story, I feel like I'm talking about another person. *Is that me?* I wonder, and I watch myself in the scenes from afar, without getting involved.

A few days after our meeting, Dr. Marnella lets me know that she sent my evaluation report to the agency.

"I'm impressed with your background," she tells me by phone, "and I think you'll be a good parent, with a very favorable support system surrounding you. I've prepared a strongly positive letter. I wish you the best in this process and a happy life with your child. Or your children."

My heart starts racing at her final comment: another mention of the possibility of twins.

What would life be like with *two* of you? Would it be any different? Would we survive the bad nights twice over?

Once Mary's and Alicia's physical and genetic studies are done, and my results are approved, the first medications will be administered to prepare Mary's uterus and stimulate Alicia's ovulation; and the doctors will give me a start date for the treatment, the egg retrieval, my sperm donation, and the transfer of the embryos. Alicia will start her injections in her hometown and then travel to San Diego for the egg retrieval.

You will be conceived in the summer.

THE FIRST ACCIDENT

JUNE II, 2004

WE ARE THE CREATORS of our nature. Without aspiring to be God, we can shape our fate. Assisted reproductive techniques are an alternative in search of perfection. Being infertile, or not having the possibility to procreate due to a biological condition or to social strictures, is a crushing differentiation that limits a person, that can destroy someone.

But assisted reproduction is complicated, emotionally. Is Mary just an organ to me? Should I see her as nothing more than a healthy young womb? And how about Alicia? Am I going to retrieve an egg from her like someone extracting bone marrow in an operating room, making her an organ donor? Well, yes . . . but no: those women are more than just organs on loan. True, we're not going to save anyone's life, we're not fighting a terrible and deadly disease, but we *are* going to create a human being. Is that not enough? I will complement myself, fill a void, eliminate a disability.

I have avoided the term *rent* throughout the entire process. There's no supply and demand market in the surrogacy business. Mary and Alicia are going to receive a payment to cover their sacrifice, their inconvenience, their absences from work or school. I'm not renting a uterus. Mary is going to help me become a dad. She is not simply a vacant room.

At this point in the seemingly endless process of manipulation, with Mary and Alicia having prepared their bodies with hormones and medications, it's finally my turn. To prepare for the donation, starting two weeks in advance I must take high doses of antibiotics. My sample has to be free of viruses or bacteria.

I buy a plane ticket to San Diego to coincide with our two-week target—the plan is to stay there for about five days. I reserve a room at a hotel in the clinic's neighborhood. This time I won't drive. Taxis and trains will be my forms of transportation.

The exact day I'm to deliver my sample depends on Alicia. Her doctor is monitoring her to see how many follicles have formed. That's where the eggs will mature. The donation is expected to result in at least eight eggs. Not all will be mature enough for use or survive the procedure, and not all will be fertilized. Later, during the transfer to the uterus (to be performed two days after the egg retrieval), others may perish. So the more follicles Alicia produces, the better—although there's always the risk of over-ovulation, which would require stopping everything and could even send her to the emergency room.

Dr. Anderson emails to let me know that they already have a frozen sample of my semen. I authorized its transfer from the Los Angeles lab to the Reproductive Sciences Center. Although sperm donation is always expected to be fresh—this increases fertilization levels—a frozen sample is kept as part of a contingency plan.

Now the question is how many embryos I should transfer to Mary's uterus. If it were up to me, I would be as aggressive as possible. Four, five, six, if possible. Dr. Anderson explains to me that two to three are usually transferred.

"We'll know more when we see the embryos," she explains.

I go to bed that night—still in New York—thinking about the beautiful babies we're going to make in the lab. I must relax, have sweet dreams, not forget Alicia's beauty and Mary's strength and total dedication. Thinking of their generosity, I manage to sleep.

I wake up with a start. I take a shower and get ready for work. At the office I receive the first sign: Alicia, I'm told, is at the clinic. "There isn't much activity so far," they tell me. She's developed only four follicles in one ovary. In the other, none. Dr. Wood says he's going to increase the dose to activate her ovulation further and see how she responds. I ask him if this is bad news and he replies, "We're going to evaluate her in two days. If there's no progress, we'll cancel the cycle."

I plead with God. I beg. I get into a subway car, sit down, and can't stop crying. I cover my face with my hands, trying to hide my helplessness as strangers avoid looking my way.

Suddenly, I feel my daughter evaporate. I stop seeing her; I stop feeling her. It's as if she's slipping out of my hands. As I exit the train and climb the stairs to the surface, I just *know* she has ceased to exist; it feels that certain.

Once again, I'm on standby, with a future I cannot trace or imagine. The antibiotics make me nauseous. Or is it the bad news? I check every second to see if a new email has arrived, but the connection is poor underground. Despite what the doctor has said, despite my lost connection with my daughter, I have not lost and will not lose hope. Why not believe in a miracle? One more day.

Above ground again, I see that Dr. Wood called me while I was on the train. I have to wait: now he's busy. Ten minutes have gone by and I'm still on the line.

"The results aren't good," he says. "The number of follicles rose to six, but they aren't large. I expected to find at least twelve. It's not an excellent cycle, not even a good one."

He tells me it's possible to up the dose to increase the stimulus. There are women who respond on the last day, but it happens in only 10 percent of the cases.

Then, yes, we'll continue trying. She could fall in that tiny percentage. I can't lose her. Her grandmother is of Spanish origin, like my grandmother. Her vulnerability fascinates me. Her eyes, her smile have captivated me. She's already part of my family. Her photos have been around the world. Everyone knows her.

We chose each other, I passed the test, and I'm not willing to suspend everything now because of a shortage of follicles. We will continue to attack, we will provoke nature; we are the ones who will write our fate. *Please, Alicia, deposit all your strength in this. Imagine that you are in control of your body, that you can produce everything you set your mind to: ten, twelve, fourteen, sixteen follicles if necessary. That's where the creation of my daughter will begin. My daughter is in your hands. Do not leave me.*

The doctor, upon further reflection, is decisive: "You must find a new donor." Mary calls me, heartbroken, when she gets the news. "Sorry, I'm so sorry," she repeats. Alicia is devastated, not only because her sacrifice has been in vain, but because she fears she won't be able to have children herself. Now she's in my shoes. It saddens me, but I don't know how to be comforting, and I don't want to be comforted either.

I disappear in the bed, among the covers and pillows. I don't want to see anyone. I just want to stop crying. I call Becca to get a new password that will allow me to access the A Perfect Match database. Yet another search, another round of trying to trust the faces of strangers.

A call from my friend Carola announces that she's becoming the mother of a one-month-old girl she adopted in New

York. The child's mother, an eighteen-year-old undocumented Mexican, decided to give her up for adoption when she found out she was pregnant. She doesn't know who the father is, nor does she wish to have contact with the child in the future. All she asked was that they tell the girl, when she grows up, to forgive her. She didn't want to say goodbye to the baby. Carola decided to call her Andrea.

HOMELESS

JUNE 12, 2004

Gonzalo and I head to Penn Station and take the train to South Orange. Traveling to New Jersey, crossing the Hudson, the border between Manhattan and the so-called Garden State, fills me with a sense of abandonment. Our life is going to change. We're going to sell our apartment and create a family in a suburb, far from the energy of the city where we've always wanted to live.

The journey seems eternal, although it's actually only twenty-five minutes. The real estate agent is waiting for us at the station. We're here to see Victorian houses in South Orange, but the station itself is far from Victorian. We imagined an old European terminal, surrounded by cafés, with a small main street full of antique shops . . . an image very distant from the reality we're witnessing.

Our agent starts us off with a tour of the city, its isolated two-story houses, its meager gardens, its empty streets. Gonzalo says that we could live there.

"Are you sure?" I ask him. "Have you seen the size of these houses?"

"At least we'll have plenty of space. And a backyard."

"Yes, a backyard we'll have to take care of. A garden that'll be covered with snow. We'll have to shovel snow to make contact with the outside world," I reply.

We walk around in colonial houses with creaky stairs and, yes, numerous halls and rooms. They've all been subdivided, and I prefer open spaces, white and bright.

We arrive at Montrose Park, the historic district. The house we see has three floors, with preserved wood paneling, stairs, and original bathrooms. It has high ceilings, and a backyard that has beguiled Gonzalo. Everything has to be in working order so that when we enter our small mansion and slam the door, it doesn't fall apart.

Back in Manhattan, Gonzalo is convinced that we should move to the house in Montrose Park. Our apartment is already for sale, and by that weekend it will be available to anyone who wants to make an offer. Everything seems to be in place.

I'd rather continue with our search, the only avenue that now makes any sense. Why would we want to get rid of our home and end up in an unknown place, with neighbors that we're not sure will accept us, in a place where sometimes the river overflows and covers the streets, reaches the houses, and destroys years of accumulated possessions. In the event of a terrible snowfall, how would we survive, with our tropical roots, having never shoveled snow or defrosted a car or driven on icy streets?

A move to Montrose Park would amount to isolating ourselves, but Gonzalo says that, with a child, we'd be isolated anyway, at least during the baby's first year of life, constantly dedicated to it. We'd have to feed it every three hours, take care of it every second, carefully observe how it breathes, sleeps, cries, smiles.

KAREN

JULY 1, 2004

I GO BACK YET AGAIN to the A Perfect Match database. I don't want to waste another minute. With every second that passes, I grow older. I'm in a pitched battle against time. I want to find a new donor instantly, free myself from the fear of losing my daughter forever.

Now the options have been reduced: the donor must be younger than twenty-five and have made a previous donation with a positive result; she must live in California—preferably in San Diego. Our chances of finding such a candidate are minimal, if not nil.

Lisa, a twenty-two-year-old Russian, has made four donations. Would she still have any eggs left? And if she does, could they have been damaged by so many hormonal treatments and medications? She's asking for twenty thousand dollars and can't undergo a cycle for another four months. She's going to France to study in the meantime. Oh God, most donors seem to want to go to Paris. Are they planning to fall in love on the banks of the Seine? Should we wait for her? Four months. That number reminds me of the previous lost four years. No, I can't wait. The other possibility is Juliet, of Italian origin.

And a Hispanic? No, I can't. I feel that it's much more diffi-cult for a Hispanic woman to let go of her child, be it a surrogate mother or an egg donor. American women are more prepared to part with the fruit of their womb, an agency assistant had whispered in my ear. In Hispanic families, children, if they ever leave, do so when they get married. American parents, on the other hand, send them off to study at eighteen, and after that the kids return home only for Thanksgiving and Christmas. I know these are just stereotypes. In fact, Elizabeth and Mary Beth, the famously remorseful surrogates, aren't Hispanic.

What's Lisa like? Should I wait for her? She has nothing that particularly draws me in. If I select her, it will be because of her IQ and her fertility level. The process keeps getting colder and more calculated. I felt a connection with Alicia; she won me over with her reasons for becoming a donor plus her Spanish grandmother.

Lisa is just . . . there, as if to say, "Take me or leave me. I'm in demand and decide who to work with. Among all the candi-dates, I will choose the one who pays me the most."

It's true: she is sought after. Not just because of the positive results of her donation, but because she's Jewish. Apparently, the only person with that background among the agency's donors. She's also the one with the fewest photos in her file: a current slightly unfocused photo and another from her childhood. None with her parents or her siblings, or from other stages in her life.

I'm not convinced. It's not a decision I can make lightly.

If someone falls in love and gets married, it's rare to wonder, before having children, about the parents' illnesses, or the grand-parents' ailments or causes of death. You're with the woman or man you love, and your fate is in the hands of the luck of the draw. When choosing the mother or father of your child, you rarely inquire about the in-laws you'll have—most will

always be a nightmare anyway—and people don't stop themselves from getting married or having children because one of
the grandparents is a curmudgeon or didn't finish elementary
school.

With an egg donor, or even a sperm donor, the scrutiny
stretches back three generations. And one tends to become de-
manding to the point of paranoia.

I don't want to reach the end of this process with that neu-
rosis. I'm not looking for a donor who resembles members of my
family or shares my ideology or religious beliefs. I'm not interested in perfection—brilliance of mind, saintly character, or a
face or figure that complies with the canons of classic beauty.

So what do I demand from the woman who will donate the
egg? That she's beautiful, smart, and healthy. That she's under
twenty-five and can provide proof of her fertility. That she's
been a donor before, and that a child has been born from the
embryos formed with her eggs. Also, for convenience, that she
lives in California.

Beauty and intelligence are relative factors anyway. After
all, my visual assessment is based on amateur photos where,
oftentimes, only one angle is visible. I wonder how each donor
walks. What her smile is like. Her hands, her feet, her ears?
Too many questions and very few answers.

As for intelligence, almost all donors go to college. Some are
enrolled in Ivy League schools and most have high test scores.
Is that enough to assess their mental power? The list includes a
Princeton graduate who has completed a master's degree and is
a third-time donor because, in addition to wanting to help an
infertile couple, she needs to pay the rent. In other words, the
degree from a prestigious university hasn't helped her get a job
that allows her to pay her most basic expenses.

Character is also tough to assess. Which donors talk incessantly, and which know how to listen? Which jump up to

free a seat on the bus for an older person? Who has the kindest heart?

Those with conditions such as kidney stones, or with mothers who wound up in the emergency room for a dislocated hip, or a grandfather who died of lung cancer as a heavy smoker are often disqualified by the agency or remain on the list of available donors for months, even years.

Once again, I'm carefully studying the smiling faces of all the young women posted, but this time—the twentieth?—Gonzalo stops me at one. Her number is 170. We open the photos, and none shows her in the pompous high school graduation gown that most choose to share. She's also not striking any erotic magazine poses or putting on suggestive expressions for what I imagine would be a captivated husband and nervous wife.

Donor 170 lives in California and is twenty-two years old. She's already been a donor, producing eighteen oocytes, thirteen of which were fertilized, although they had to be reserved because the gestational mother wasn't ready on time. The pregnancy was positive and twins were born from the frozen embryos. Her physical attributes are good: she's tall and slim, with astonishing light-blue eyes.

Her name is Karen. She came from a Slavic country to the United States as a child with her family, and they settled in California. She's the youngest of her siblings. She speaks English and her native language, and studies art and international law in college.

Someone in her family, or perhaps it was she herself—it's unspecified—was under psychiatric treatment, apparently for depression. She drinks alcohol twice a week, almost always with friends, during dinner. She doesn't do drugs but has some tattoos and some body piercings.

She's not perfect, she's not the ideal donor, but at least I sense that she's not lying. I find her profile interesting; however, she gives us the distinct impression of being a rebel without a cause. We're a little alarmed by that, so we return to her photos and her answers to the agency's extensive questionnaire.

The more I look at her, the more I see her as beautiful. She's undoubtedly the least conventional donor in the database. Why, then, has she not been reserved, like so many others? She's smart—at least it seems so—beautiful, twenty-two, and a candidate with proven fertility. Could it be the tattoos and piercings that put people off? Or because someone in her family suffered from depression? Or maybe because she's European?

In any case, all those doubts are in my favor. So far, Karen is our first and, apparently, only choice.

Becca tells us that there's a couple before us who are also interested in Karen. We'll have to wait for them to make a decision. "Karen is a doll," says Becca, unaware that it spikes my anxiety even further.

"I think I'm going to drive myself crazy, Becca. We're not interested in anyone else from your database. If it's not Karen, I'll have to start looking at other agencies, or even stop the whole process."

Unable to help myself, I go back to the bio: Karen is very sociable, highly motivated, and always demands the best from herself. She's also relaxed, knows how to enjoy her free time, and likes everything related to art. In her spare time, she paints— mostly abstract works.

Her goals are to become a lawyer, to continue painting, and to sell her paintings one day. She likes to read, go to modern art museums, and spend time with her friends and family. She wants to be a donor because she takes pleasure in helping families who can't have children. She doesn't have a boyfriend, and her friends will support her in the donation process. She currently takes

birth control pills and has been menstruating since she was fifteen, every twenty-eight days, for four days. As far as she knows,
there's no genetic disease in her family.

Her maternal grandfather died very young in an accident,
and of her paternal grandparents, one died of cancer in his seven-
ties and the other in her eighties of a heart attack. The maternal
grandmother is still alive.

Karen has never been involved in a lawsuit or in situations
that could put her at risk of contracting sexually transmitted diseases. She was raised in a Catholic family and is convinced that
egg donation is consistent with both her beliefs and her ethics.
She's not concerned about the risks involved in donating. In fact,
she tolerated the injections and blood tests without any issues
last time around.

As for the baby she's going to help create, she's aware that it
won't belong to her. What she does ask is that the unused frozen
embryos be destined for medical research, and that they not be
donated to others for the purpose of conceiving a second or third
baby.

I review the psychological test that she underwent for her
first donation. She's never had any eating, drug, or alcohol problems. She was prescribed antidepressants to help her through
a difficult few months, but her depressed state appears to have
been situational, the analysis clarifies.

The psychologist concluded that Karen is an intelligent,
focused, independent, and charismatic girl. Despite her young
age—the American Society for Reproductive Medicine (ASRM)
has a guideline requiring donors to be at least twenty-one years
old—she demonstrates a high level of maturity and clearly understands the short- and long-term implications of egg donation. In
conclusion, the psychologist recommended Karen for donation.

What else do we need to know? Gonzalo and I go back to

the database for the zillionth time, and no one else catches our eye. We want Karen. I send her pictures to my mother and sister, and they're delighted. Karen must be the one to donate the egg to have you, Emma. I have to put all my energy to work for that to happen.

Becca gets in touch to tell me that the couple who have Karen on reserve are unable to decide quickly. They need more time, so they prefer to allow Karen to be available to others. Furthermore, she's read our profile and wants to work with us. She's ours! I let Gonzalo know. I offer six thousand dollars and she accepts.

The decision is final: Karen will provide the necessary cell to create you, Emma. The moment of meeting you is inching closer.

Next up: selling the apartment. We start showing it, and the response to the sale announcement is enormous. Several interested parties come check it out, many like it, and we get our first offer. Apparently, it's going to be sold ahead of schedule.

KM V. EG

Every time I fly to Los Angeles, I try to stay at the Mondrian Hotel. It's perfectly located on Sunset Boulevard, close to the photography studios where we set up the *People en Español* cover shoots and a short distance from my friend Carmen, who also works for the magazine.

Carmen goes above and beyond when hosting dinners, making them feel more like family gatherings than work meetings. With her unique grace, she mingles her relatives with magazine editors and clients inside a cozy home that she herself has decorated down to the smallest detail.

Carmen knows that I'm looking to have a baby—actually, everyone knows it by now—and this time she wants me to meet two of her close friends who have already gone through the same process. Robert and Karl have two girls; one is two years old and the other is five months old. They arrive with a nanny who takes care of the toddler. I discover that we share the same attorney, that they also started with Growing Generations, and that they likewise ended up choosing another agency.

"Get ready: it's not going to be easy. Now, with the girls here and part of the family, I've sort of forgotten everything we went through," says Robert. "The first time, a blood test revealed that the gestational mother was pregnant: the numbers were high, but . . . nothing. We have a friend whose surrogate mother lost her baby when she was five months pregnant. Anyway, you have to be ready for anything."

And how can I not be? Preparation began in another era— that's how long I've been gearing up. One day I was declared infertile. Four years later, the doctor told me I could have children. But then my first egg donor didn't produce enough follicles. I share all this with Robert and Karl, unable to hold back my tears. I change the subject and we talk about their life with the girls: the bad nights, how they want to move to Tennessee (where they already bought a house to be close to their family).

"I want my daughters to grow up surrounded by their grandparents, their aunts, their cousins," says Robert.

The next day, while at a breakfast with my editor and a talent agent at the Chateau Marmont hotel, I receive a message from my lawyer telling me that he must speak with me urgently. I excuse myself and call him, and within seconds I lose all focus: there's a case in the California Supreme Court, KM v. EG, that could set a negative precedent for all surrogacy processes.

KM and EG are a lesbian couple. In March 2001, KM filed a petition to establish her maternal rights over the twin girls that EG had had about five years earlier. Her petition was denied. Now the case has been considered and decided by the California Supreme Court. KM alleges that she's the biological mother of the girls, as she provided the egg that was fertilized in vitro and transferred to EG's uterus.

Meanwhile, EG wants to enforce the legal agreement signed by KM before egg donation—a document in which the latter relinquished the rights to any children born from her donated eggs.

EG testified that she had considered being a single mother even before meeting KM in 1992. She had told KM that she wanted to adopt a child, she'd initiated the application, and they'd registered their domestic partnership in San Francisco.

In 1993, EG visited multiple fertility clinics and made several attempts at artificial insemination, to no avail. KM accompanied her to these medical appointments and, as she later assured the judge, they both intended to raise, together, the child or children who would be born. EG claims the contrary: her intention was to be a single mother.

In 1994, EG began in vitro fertilization, which failed because she didn't produce enough eggs. The following year, KM agreed to become a donor on the condition, according to EG, that EG would be the only mother of the children, and that she would not allow KM to legally adopt them until they were at least five years old and she felt that the relationship was stable. They agreed not to reveal to anyone that KM had been the donor of the oocyte. They then selected the sperm donor together.

KM denies that the idea was for EG to be a single mother from the outset and claims that she wouldn't have agreed to be a donor under those circumstances. However, a four-page document signed by her maintains otherwise. In that document, part of the egg donation paperwork, KM relinquished all rights, both to the donated eggs and to any children born from them. EG claims that she discussed the document with KM and wouldn't have accepted the eggs if KM hadn't signed the document.

The embryos resulting from KM's eggs were implanted in EG in April 1995. The girls were born in December of that year, and their birth certificate shows that their mother is EG, not KM. Shortly after becoming a mom, EG asked KM to marry her, and they exchanged rings over Christmas. None of their relatives, their friends, or their pediatrician knew that KM was the genetic mother of the girls. EG included the babies in her health insurance, increased her life insurance, and declared the twins as her beneficiaries. KM did none of these things. However, the nursemaids who worked for them stated that they considered both KM and EG to be the mothers of the twins.

The couple's relationship ended in March 2001. That's when KM began her legal battle. By September, EG had moved to Massachusetts with the girls to live with her mother.

The California Supreme Court recognized the document signed by KM as valid, concluding that she donated genetic material without any intention of becoming the mother of the children created from her eggs. In addition, it ruled that KM didn't qualify as a parent because there was substantial evidence to indicate that the only *intentional* mother was EG, who from the beginning aimed to raise the babies alone. The court made it clear that KM was considered to fall under the same terms as a sperm donor.

How could this resolution affect me? My lawyer explains that he believes this case sets a precedent: a gestational mother has been granted the rights to a child conceived in her womb with different genetic material from her own. In other words, the *intention* of being a mother is paramount

EG wasn't a gestational mother by circumstance. She carried children conceived by sperm and egg donors in her womb; but from the beginning, as the legal documents indicate, she was the only one who intended to be a mother. According to my lawyer, for future legal reference, it's good to note that maternity rights have been granted to a surrogate mother.

I don't think this precedent will jeopardize my existing legal agreements with Mary and Karen. Mary has relinquished maternal rights over the child soon to be in her womb, as KM did over her eggs. Likewise, Karen will donate eggs over whose fruit she doesn't want any legal rights. My situation is the same as EG's. From my point of view, that ruling from the California Supreme Court protects me. For the lawyer, it's an established precedent that could lead to several unknowns.

I go back to breakfast and everyone is surprised by my look of consternation. It's nothing, I say; I don't want to go into details. I don't even want to think about details. Instead, I try to relegate that conversation with my lawyer into oblivion.

I fly back to New York, once again besieged by doubts.

THE CONNECTION

I DON'T BELIEVE IN LUCK, at least not in good luck. In the past, my days have been conditioned by whether I got out of bed with my right or my left foot. I've learned that I can control which foot I get up with—and that's about the extent of my control.

Good luck is relative. I instigate it, guide it. What I know clearly is that nothing falls from the sky. There are those who are born with good luck, or so they say. I have to work for it, lift it brick by brick, and avoid any mistakes to keep it from collapsing. It's not that I'm unlucky; quite the contrary. I just feel that each achievement involves a long journey of vicissitudes.

Today, before getting up, I stop to think with which foot I should start the day. *Right*, I decide. Today, I want everything to go well for me. We finally—I try to convince myself—have Karen, we finally have Mary; everything is ready for "operation baby."

But I feel a need to know more about Karen. Although the agency backs the information about their donors—they check to see if each one has a criminal record, they do a genetic test—I don't know what her life is like or what her tastes are beyond the expected questionnaire answers. I know that Karen is in college and I know her country of origin, I also know how many siblings she has. I know the high school she went to; I know she lives in California, is twenty-two years old, and has already been an egg donor. It's enough to start my research. Dozens of Karens turn up on the internet. I whittle down the selection until, to my surprise, I find her sooner than expected. In this age of cyber–social connections, no one can hide. The phrase "it's like looking for a needle in a haystack" has become obsolete. If you're looking for something, you will find it.

On a website that mainly posts student opinions, Karen is an open book. She posts a journal, typically updating it more than once a month but sometimes not writing a single word for two or three months.

From her postings, I verify that, in addition to her tattoos, she indeed has body piercings. At times I feel like a father whose daughter, who has been educated in private schools and goes to mass every Sunday, shows up at the house tattooed and covered with piercings. What do you do? Get angry? At the end of the day, she's your daughter. Karen, in this case, will be the "mother" of my daughter. There's no turning back.

She likes rock. She's a passionate fan of the Cure, Led Zeppelin, and Pat Benatar. I want to listen to the music she enjoys, to know the tastes of the woman who is going to contribute 50 percent of my daughter's genetic material. Her favorite movies include *Amélie*, *Lost in Translation*, *Fear and Loathing in Las Vegas*, *Reservoir Dogs*, and *Breakfast at Tiffany's*. At least she has good cinematic taste. She also claims to be a devourer of books.

Among her favorite visual artists is Ana Mendieta: I finally find a connection with her! There will soon be an Ana Mendieta retrospective at the Whitney Museum in New York. I'll buy the catalog for her. Maybe we'll be able to talk about our common artistic tastes.

Should I mention them to her? Should I let her know that I've seen her adventures in cyberspace? No, I better give her the catalog the day she makes the donation. It will be a justified gift, because I know that she studies art, because I'm Cuban, because Ana Mendieta is Cuban.

I keep reading. Karen likes to paint in her spare time, she loves the eighties culture, and she can't live without Vietnamese food and green beans. She's happy when surrounded by artists; she also enjoys leaving the city on weekends, dancing at parties, eating sushi, and falling in love with intensity. Lying makes her sad; she dislikes opportunistic friends, disrespectful men, being uninspired, boredom, failure, "love" in quotes, regretting things she has done, and Tom.

Who is Tom? Will I be able to find *him* in this puzzle? Karen and Tom. I resume the search. Something else has to pop up. I scroll through her journal but find nothing. I'll have to leave it for another day. At some point his identity will come out. At least I know that Tom didn't leave her with any fond memories.

Is this the kind of woman I want? Have I taken the right step? I know she's an intelligent young person. Beautiful, without a doubt. Interesting, of course. Too shrewd . . . perhaps? A bit aggressive, rebellious? What traits will my daughter inherit from her? And what are we looking for exactly? Of all the women in the agency's database, she's the only one since Alicia I've felt a real connection with; someone who, in turn, never ceases to intrigue me. At least we'll be able to exchange a few words about the artists we like: Whiteread's casts and Hirst's quartered animals in formaldehyde that we both recently saw at the Brooklyn Museum; or Abakanowicz's performance in Chelsea, where she lived for several days in a gallery and we saw her bathe, eat, dress, sleep. We could also talk about Mendieta's installation in a ceiba tree on Eighth Street in Miami, or when I met her during a visit to Cuba; or discuss how the artist fell to her death—or was thrown, as some think—from her SoHo apartment window. We have a lot to talk about. Someday.

And one day my daughter will also discover these artists. She'll understand our tastes and know why I selected Karen, why I traced our fate with a Baltic woman. And like Czesław Miłosz, Karen's favorite poet, I'll "lament my foolish ways, but even if I had been wise, I would have failed to change my fate. I lament my foolishness then and later and now, for which I would like so much to be forgiven."

THE SECOND ACCIDENT

AUGUST 2004

A WEEK BEFORE MARY BEGINS the medication cycle to prep her for the embryo transfer, I lose contact with her. I leave messages on her phone and send several emails but receive no response. I contact the agency and ask how she's doing. They tell me that she attended the most recent monthly surrogacy meeting and that they'll contact her as soon as possible.

I begin to panic, as I do every time I'm about to start a new stage of this process. Or rather, each time I finish a search, an investigative stage. When the moment of truth arrives, I'm gripped by restlessness.

Karen has already had the very expensive injections to start ovarian stimulation and thus encourage the follicular phase. Based on our experience with Alicia, Karen has to produce at least ten follicles. The key is for the respective hormonal processes of both the donor and the surrogate mother to be synchronized so that the implant takes place seamlessly. Timing the egg donation and uterus preparation is essential.

Is Mary having second thoughts? She's under contract, but she hasn't received any money yet. Until the pregnancy is confirmed, she won't get the twenty-thousand-dollar payment allocated in monthly installments. Is she sick? I get an email from Dr. Wood's office. I must decide if I'm willing to continue even if Mary isn't ready. If the egg donation proceeds, enough mature eggs are obtained, and we conceive the embryos, these could be preserved until we're ready for the transfer.

I begin to send Mary messages of despair, including a postcard in the mail. I'm teetering on the brink of calling her work, her mother. If Mary cancels, we'll have to find another surrogate mother, and by then, my energy will be depleted. I can't waste a second. I've already lost four years! I enter the Surrogate Alternatives database and scan through carriers, but the options are minimal. The agency tells me that they've phoned Mary, that they've left her messages but haven't heard back. Has she gone on a trip? Is her little girl sick?

If Karen is willing to continue, I'm not going to stop her. The donation process could get tougher later, with her college courses. The hardest part is this synchronization, getting both of the women to be at the same place in their menstrual cycle practically at the same time. And just when we're close to succeeding, Mary disappears.

Trained to calm desperate people—I can imagine intentional mothers and fathers mired in anguish when something goes wrong—Melinda notes that we still have time.

"Let's wait for the weekend," she suggests. "One of the surrogate mothers in the group is going to try to visit her on Saturday."

That means another three days of waiting. At least we'll have an answer by Saturday. What if she's not home, though? What if Mary decided to abandon everything and move to Israel, where her father's family lives?

Meanwhile, Gonzalo and I accept an offer to buy the apartment. Getting the board's approval on closing can take months, but we're making progress.

At long last, I get a call from Mary. Her daughter threw the cell phone into the toilet, she explains. She didn't have time to drive to a store to replace it until today, but they've just now activated a new one. Making matters worse, her computer is broken. She doesn't want to sound irresponsible, she says, but it's been very difficult to work and take care of her three-year-old without any help. Also, things with her daughter's father "aren't going well."

I don't ask about what's happening with her partner, but I wonder: Will there be a separation? Mary is under a great deal of stress now, right before starting the preparatory phase. She should be relaxed for the day of the transfer, after which she must be on bed rest for twenty-four hours. That means she can't even go to the bathroom: she must remain in bed. Nothing could be untimelier than being upset with her daughter's father.

However, these issues don't seem to affect her. Her voice and slow-paced tone convey a sense of calm. She's silent while waiting for my response. She sighs and begins to speak again. I interrupt her and jump in with questions, because I have to rid myself of the uncertainty. If we're to move forward, all doubts must be dispelled.

"Do you want to wait awhile? A few months?" I ask, mentally begging for her to say no. Two months would be like two years. "Do you want us to stop everything, Mary, so you can think about it?"

"I'm ready. Do *you* want to stop?" She answers with a question, without mentioning what I want to hear: that she *wants* to start the process, that she wants it very much, that it's the most important thing for her, that she'll have the support of her family, that she'll be relaxed.

"So, should we start?" I ask, giving her another chance to say what I'm hoping for.

Her answer boils down to a monosyllable. "Yes."

A simple yes. Ah, Mary, the time has come. There's nothing else to look or hope for. Now she just has to get in touch with the doctors and Surrogate Alternatives. When her cycle and Karen's have been synchronized, she'll begin to inject the hormones that will prepare her uterus to host the beautiful embryos that Karen and I will produce.

That weekend, Gonzalo and I head over to the Whitney Museum, to the newly arrived Ana Mendieta exhibition: scenes of violence, works made with blood, her naked body on the ground, performances. Seeing her work together in one place allows the viewer to perceive the overwhelming premonition of her death. I buy the catalog to give to Karen on donation day.

Now I wait for the call from Dr. Wood, who will be evaluating Karen before giving the go-ahead for her to continue the cycle. At least she's experienced. If she previously produced sixteen oocytes, how many will she make now? The same amount?

"I think you should look for another egg donor," is the doctor's first sentence. Straight to the point. My legs are shaking. My already substantial debt will rise. I'll have to enter the database again.

"Something is wrong," he continues. "Someone is lying."

Oh God, what happened now? What new obstacle will I have to overcome?

Then he drops a bombshell. "Karen is pregnant."

Silence. Nothing else is said on the other end of the line. I too say nothing. What do you do in a situation like this? I've read about every possible mishap in assisted reproduction, but I've never seen anything about the possibility of the egg donor becoming pregnant.

Who's the father? I wonder. She signed a legal contract by

which she agreed to abstain from sexual intercourse during the period of ovulation induction. Also, how did she dare have unprotected sex? How could the agency list such a careless person?

"The choice is yours. I don't know how much you can trust her, though," the doctor declares. "If, however, you insist on working with Karen because she's the donor you want, we'll have to wait three months after she terminates the pregnancy to begin another cycle."

All that money lost. Injections, doctor visits, ultrasounds, blood tests. And now, what do I tell Mary, who is ready, who has even talked to her mother about helping her with her daughter during the cycle?

Becca from A Perfect Match doesn't understand how something like this could have happened.

"She's a serious young woman," she assures me. But that means nothing. Karen has breached the contract. Not only did she have sex, but she didn't protect herself. "I spoke to her a few minutes ago, and she sounded sincere."

She has just realized she's pregnant, Becca explains. If she has an abortion, we'll have to wait only six weeks for the next cycle.

That doesn't sound so bad, but it contradicts Dr. Wood's three-month recommendation when he broke the news. He explained then that it wouldn't be wise to continue with a cycle immediately after, since a termination can reduce the production of follicles.

Another decision I must make. Becca forwards me the email she received from Karen, in which she apologizes and is very sorry to have caused the situation we're all in. She already has an appointment with her gynecologist to end her unexpected pregnancy. Once she's ready, she'll do everything in her power to complete a cycle for me, if I'm willing to give her a second chance. She asks how I feel and sends me her deepest apologies. Nothing will make her happier than continuing with me, she writes, and she's open to meeting in person and keeping me up to date on the whole process.

I can't stop to analyze the consequences or delay the decision too long. There's nothing else to think about.

We will continue with Karen.

RETURNING TO MIAMI

OCTOBER 2004

E VERYTHING CAN CHANGE IN a second.
Today I get out of bed—on the right foot?—and decide
to talk to Richard, my boss. Once the apartment sale is finalized, our options will be limited to moving outside of the city.

Maybe I should take a year's leave of absence, move with
Gonzalo to Miami, dedicate myself to the baby, and then re-
think my future. At the end of the day, it's my fate, I remind myself. I must build it. My mom, sister, cousins, and many friends
are in Miami.

Getting a two-bedroom apartment in the city on my budget isn't possible, but for the same price, I could buy a house in
Miami. I could even rent a place to live in during that first year
and then decide whether or not to return to New York.

Nobody at the magazine knows I'm considering this. No one
in my family even imagines this option. To be honest, I haven't
discussed it thoroughly with Gonzalo, but I'm increasingly convinced that it's the best thing for the baby, for us. After such
sacrifices to become a father, not being able to be with my child
during his or her early years doesn't make sense.

But will the company allow it? They can't deny me a year's leave without salary; there are several editors who have already done this. Plus, I've been working for the magazine for seven years; it's time to take a break from interviews, conceiving covers, editing.

I phone Richard, my boss, to make my case. He listens dumbfounded.

I figure the discussion will have no immediate response, as the decision will presumably have to be made in consultation with others in the company. I've also thought about staying on as a consultant or to manage exclusive assignments, but I'm not ready for the option my editor offers me.

"Move to Miami," he says after a moment, "but don't go on leave. Work from home and come to New York once a month."

He takes me totally by surprise. Should I accept? Or wait until tomorrow, after I've talked with Gonzalo?

"Sounds like a good idea," I reply gratefully, "but trips to New York will have to wait until the baby—once there is one—is at least four months old."

My mother can't believe it. Gonzalo, who thought the possibility of returning to Miami was remote, is taken aback.

Now we have to start looking for a house in Miami. We browse the real estate pages for available properties within our budget; my sister and mom check them out and send us photos. We book tickets to Miami for the following weekend. There are no seconds to waste. That's how I begin to imagine your room, Emma, painted a light color—not pink, not blue—the rays of sunlight through your window, the backyard view, your white crib. We're leaving New York, the city where we had always dreamed of living, to return to Miami.

And I realize that, in that instant, my life has changed once more.

MEETING KAREN

NOVEMBER 18, 2004

E VERY TIME SUMMER COMES to an end, I'm happy. Fall, winter, and spring are the seasons of the year that I prefer. Summer turns New York into a sewer, so when the trees start to
lose their leaves, I feel like my life is about to change seasons
too. However, in October my vulnerability usually takes over.
Perhaps because I'm a Libra—my birthday is in October, and
with it comes evidence that I'm growing old—and because the
important things in my life always seem to happen at the end
of the year. I left Cuba on October 1 many years ago; we moved
back to Miami in October and bought the house where we're
preparing our nest. On November 3, 1997, I moved to New York
and started working at the magazine, and this November 18 I
met Karen. We're back on: she will donate her eggs at the end
of this month.

I read and reread the email Karen had sent me through
Becca a few days earlier. Did her words make me want to work
with her again? I don't think so. However, they confirmed that I
hadn't made the wrong decision. Even before reading that message, I was convinced that if she was willing to commit to doing

another cycle with me, even if I had to wait for her for three months, it was worth it.

My energy was on the verge of depletion; I didn't have the strength to start another search at that point—to turn strangers into familiar faces, pass another test, get another approval. I had already come part of the way with Karen, and I didn't want to retrace my steps.

I added only one condition, in response to her email: I wanted to get to know her; I wanted us to meet. She accepted instantly, although she had some fears: Would I be very angry? Would I seek some sort of revenge for her irresponsibility, for the money and time she had made me lose?

If there's one thing I'm sure of, it's that I'm not vindictive, but meeting a man twice her age, who was about to violate the usual barriers of anonymity that egg donation entails, posed a bit of a dilemma. So Karen also inquired about me. Becca reassured her, gave her confidence. The meeting had to take place in a public space, Becca advised, so she could feel safe. Also, it should be in her city. Taking her out of her environment might create more doubts.

DURING THE FLIGHT, Gonzalo and I try to imagine how Karen will receive us. While Mary was relaxed and calm, perhaps Karen will be imposing and active. We'll get to discover her tattoos, her style. Gonzalo thinks maybe she's into goth fashion, while I imagine her more as an out-of-date hippie, or maybe a rocker. But she could also be a mistimed Madonna. Didn't her profile say that she loves the eighties?

We imagine her in jeans, boots, and a sexy red or orange blouse. Does she have long hair? We'll soon find out if the photos she has on her A Perfect Match page are current.

The best thing about this meeting is that now Karen will be the one trying to convince *me* to work with *her*. I feel a little more in control, because I'm not the one taking the test. The person being evaluated, this time, is Karen. To proceed, I'll have to benefit in some way from her mistake—a mistake that perhaps was actually a sign warning me that I had to meet her, that I shouldn't commit myself to accepting her genetic code without first hearing her voice, observing her gestures, and contemplating her gaze. Perhaps—we'll find out—the accident had to happen to convince me that I should look for another donor. Had Karen been simply a hindrance of fate? No, *I* shape fate: *I* get to decide whether Karen will be there or not.

I fall asleep during the flight. Gonzalo is anxious, lost in thought. He can't even close his eyes. He's afraid of flying (or was then), which doesn't help.

We arrive at the hotel, located in the city center, late in the day and have dinner in the same spot where breakfast with Karen will take place the next day. I want to familiarize myself with our terrain. We go to the room early.

The meeting is set for nine in the morning. Karen requested that time so she could make her afternoon classes. She has to cross the city and will encounter more traffic than usual in the morning, so she asked in advance for our patience.

We go down to the hotel lobby at eight thirty, just in case she's early. Gonzalo, of course, has the camera ready. Will she let us take her picture? Maybe video, we have to record a video. After all, this will be the only encounter with the woman who will contribute half of our baby's genes.

As the time draws near, we became more aware of the momentousness of the occasion. We're going to see our future daughter in Karen, be able to imagine what our little girl will look like at twenty-two.

Even Karen's voice is an object of great curiosity. "What if she has a nasal or high-pitched voice that bothers us from the moment she starts to speak?" I say to Gonzalo. I'm not too worried about the rest. The photos are there; I've seen her. Besides, she's going to contribute only 50 percent of the genetic mix.

Sitting on one of the hotel lobby's lush velvet sofas, I search for Karen in every woman who walks by. I feel ridiculous on that rococo piece of furniture that gives my waiting an even more dramatic air. I try to make eye contact with each woman who enters. Some even hold my gaze, puzzled. Karen could be any of them. Until my phone rings.

"I'm not going to make it on time," Karen says brusquely. "I think it'll take another thirty minutes. There's a lot of traffic."

Direct, blunt, with no room for apologies. That's that. She doesn't even ask if we can wait for her. Of *course* we're going to be there for her—one, two, three hours, all day if necessary. We crossed the country for an encounter that will remain forever etched in my memory. She speaks to me like an executive about to make a presentation: take it or leave it. We both need each other, but in the end, she knows that I need her more than she needs me. One intentional parent less or more won't affect her. After all, before I selected her, there was already a couple who had reserved her services and who couldn't use them as quickly as I was willing to. She may even sense my despair now.

"See you," she says, ending the exchange. I don't think she even waits for me to say goodbye. I feel like I did when standing in front of my first-grade teacher during a scolding. Karen is clearly in control. The funny thing is that I'd dared to think *I* was in control.

Nervous? Not at all. I never imagined she'd show such confidence. And her voice? Clear and well rounded. Fortunately, not the voice of many young women her age who use a tone that depicts them as both childish and sensual. Luckily, not a Barbie voice.

I can breathe easy. I don't care if she speaks to me as if I were the one making her wait. Maybe she figures that, since I plucked her out of her routine and made her drive to the other end of town before class, I can wait.

Now, having heard her voice and her confidence, I revise my expectations of her appearance. I'm guessing she'll be dressed to portray an image that has nothing to do with her own, that she'll have left her school attire behind to present herself the way a future father might expect of a woman who will be donating the first cell to create his child.

At long last, she enters the lobby, wearing a loose cream-colored overcoat and a tight-fitting black blouse and pants ensemble, exhibiting full control of the terrain. We recognize each other instantly. She approaches me and establishes distance by stretching out her arm and firmly shaking my hand. Then she smiles. She smiles as only she can, revealing perfect white teeth—which is natural, since her file says that she never had to wear braces—and with her hand, in a very feminine gesture, she brushes her hair away from her face and tucks it behind her ear. It's as if she's uncovering her face for me, knowing that I'm going to evaluate her, that I want to examine every line of her countenance.

She isn't wearing any makeup, except for black eyeliner flush with her upper lashes, highlighting the imposing color of her eyes. Her very light eyebrows are plucked to perfection and follow the natural line of her eyes. Her lips are a natural pink. On her long neck rests a thin gold necklace. She doesn't wear perfume. Her hair is cut straight above her shoulders.

Although I already knew her height, having her next to us is striking: she's definitely tall. I cast a discreet glance down to see if she's wearing high heels, but notice that she has on low-heeled black boots.

"Sorry for the delay," she says.

I wasn't expecting an apology from her. I thought I was the one who should apologize for having interrupted her routine. I, the intentional father desperate to receive the wonderful egg that will have her genetic code; she, an intelligent woman of exceptional beauty and intelligence with a confident, clear, and beautiful voice.

"Don't worry," I say to hide my anxiety. I'm sure she senses that I want to devour her with questions. I'm captivated by her smile, her gaze, the warmth and firmness of her handshake (the only physical contact she grants me).

As I enter the restaurant, I dare to gently place my arm on her shoulder, almost imperceptibly. I think I make contact only with her cashmere overcoat, which she takes off without help before placing her leather bag on the floor. I take in her slim body, small waist, long legs, straight hips. Then she opens the menu.

"What are you going to order?" she asks.

This woman is incredible. She knows she's in control. Without waiting for my response, she signals to the waiter and orders coffee, orange juice, scrambled eggs, and toast. I smile and ask for the same.

"I want you to know that I'm very sorry for what we've been through."

What? She's speaking in the plural? It seems that I too was to blame for her getting pregnant, when *she* was the one who breached the contract and had sex in the middle of the cycle. She knew all too well—and could attest to it—that injections and pills to aggressively stimulate her reproductive system would make her more fertile. What did she expect? That's the only reason she subjected herself to a barrage of hormones, right?

"I didn't look for it," she says. "It was an accident that has left us all in a bad position."

Wait, what's she talking about? *Exclude me from your mistake, Karen, please. I'm a victim of your irresponsibility.* The thousands of questions I harbor make me feel like I'm about to burst, but I manage only a meaningless phrase: "Don't worry, those things happen."

Nonetheless, she forges ahead with her apology, her convincing voice, her captivating eyes, her charming smile. Meanwhile, I want to ask about her, about her family, about growing up in a Baltic country.

"I want it to work this time," she assures us. "I guarantee that everything will be fine, and I thank you for deciding to continue with me."

At last I sense she's on my side. *Yes, of course I want to continue with you!* I feel like yelling this to her, but I hold back. I'd like to tell her that I'm fascinated by her way of speaking, of taking control of a situation that put her at a disadvantage and rising above it with the conviction that mistakes are to be left in the past and that one must forgive. *I know how to forgive, Karen.*

When I address her as Karen, even if only in my thoughts, the name finally becomes real to me; it's no longer just a key used to enter a database where women expose their genetic history.

As Karen begins to eat, she leans forward, lengthens her neck, and suddenly appears vulnerable. My turn has come.

I ask her to tell us about herself. She has no accent in English because she came with her parents when she was very young, she tells us. She has returned to her country several times. The most recent trip was last year, to celebrate her grandmother's seventieth birthday. She likes going back, but her life is in California.

She's afraid of big cities. She dreams of one day taking her paintings to a gallery in Los Angeles, but she doesn't know if she could survive that city's dynamics, the people's energy. She tells me that she's never visited New York or Miami. I tell her that when she does, she should look us up. She smiles, and I hear the answer she doesn't utter: *That will never happen; this will be the only time we meet.*

I ask her to tell me about her paintings. "They're abstract," she says succinctly.

Then I tell her about me, about our first accident with Alicia, the previous donor. And she smiles again, this time with an expression that could be translated as a combination of "Sorry" and "It's a good thing that happened, because now we're going to work together."

As time passes, I start to see the real Karen. She loses her confidence; her eyes and smile reveal her hidden fragility, her fears, her loneliness. Yes, I see her alone in a room with her dogs—she loves animals passionately; every time she sees an abandoned dog, she adopts it until she finds it a good family—unburdening herself on a blank canvas, furiously staining it with red and black.

Karen still doesn't know where her life is going. I see her far from her family and imagine her enjoying every minute of her independence. But there's so much I don't know. What was her childhood like? Does she regret fleeing her country and leaving family and school friends behind? How did her parents' divorce affect her? Did her decision to study in another city infuriate her mother, who couldn't adapt to the idea that her daughter was away from home? Or did her mother have to dedicate all her time to work and fail to give her enough attention?

For example, what about Tom, whom she mentioned disliking in her journal? Perhaps she feels disregarded by him; or is she still in love with him and simply can't get over him? Is Tom the one who caused the pregnancy accident, forcing her to get rid of her fetus because at that point in her life the last thing she needed was to further complicate it?

Since I'm now in control of the conversation, I decide to mention one of my favorite artists: Ana Mendieta. She may suspect that I found her own interest in Mendieta on some personal website and think that I was prying too deeply into her private life, but she has to know that privacy in cyberspace is an illusion. In the end, I don't care if that's what she thinks: it would only go to show that my interest in her is serious, and that I'm unwilling to tolerate another mistake. In any case, it's easy to get to that topic: Karen is passionate about art, Ana was Cuban, me too. I start from the Mendieta retrospective at the Whitney. I even encourage her to go to New York, because it's a unique opportunity.

But Karen doesn't confirm that Mendieta is one of her favorite artists. She tells me that her work had been a subject of one of the courses she had just taken, and that she had been struck by Mendieta's level of physical commitment to her pieces. The body becomes part of the discourse, I note; she is, herself, her work. All of Mendieta's pieces reveal the idea of a fragmented identity. Her childhood, her exile; the sacrificial rituals, which become political in Mendieta's gaze. We also talk about her pieces made in Mexico. Karen loves *Mutilated Body on Landscape* and expresses this to me somewhat timidly, as if the title of the work were to give her away. It's clear that she doesn't want to show herself in a multidimensional way. She just hopes that I'll see her beautiful face and the results of her genetic tests.

But I insist on going further. She quickly realizes who's in control now, and I subtly let her know that I have no intention of losing it, at least not in front of her. We then speak of the skin-deep violence and death in all of Mendieta's work. Finally we came to the harshness of *Rape Scene*, *Feathers on a Woman*, and *Death of a Chicken*, in which Mendieta stars in images where the nakedness, blood, and mutilation hit the viewer like a slap in the face.

Karen looks like a student now. Moving on from art, I want to probe the motives, both altruistic and financial, that led her to donate part of her body without caring about possible long-term side effects, whether infertility, cancer, an infection that could cause death, or an excessive ovulation that could send her to the emergency room.

She becomes more and more vulnerable before my eyes. I see her helplessness, and I also perceive that her beauty serves as a protective shield. As I get to know her better, that shield begins to crumble.

On a sensory level, she's captivated me with her face. From the beginning of time, beauty has been associated with goodness: now I'm sure that Karen will take care of herself, and that her body will be ready to produce the perfect cells that I need.

Gonzalo and I accompany her to the hotel's exit, and this time we hug goodbye. With my arm around her shoulders, as if to protect her, I feel that she's smaller despite her height. On the sidewalk, Gonzalo tells her that we'd like to photograph her, and she seems a little taken aback. She moves to my side, still smiling. I slide my arm around her waist, and she poses for a few seconds. She then draws apart and walks away, hinting that she isn't comfortable with the camera. Gonzalo manages to record a few seconds as she wanders off.

She walks slowly, with her head down, as if trying to avoid tripping. She knows we're watching her, maybe thinks we're following her with the camera, but we aren't. She doesn't look back. Those few yards must be an eternity for her.

While waiting for the light to change so that she can walk

to the other side of the street, she crosses her arms and draws her shoulders in as if she were cold. When she turns to the side to check for traffic, I see that she retains her soft smile. Even at that distance, I understand what she later calls her "moody eyes, droopy eyelids," which she says my daughter inherited from her. I'm overcome by her fragility. Seeing her leave fills me with sadness.

As she reaches the next corner, she quickens her pace. I look one last time at her profile. It's like watching a scene in a video that I want to pause. Against my will, she moves on.

Then, she turns her face to me without making eye contact, head still down, smiling. She closes her eyes, as if wanting to say goodbye to me, and then disappears around a city corner.

I would never see her again.

THE MIRACLES

NOVEMBER 30, 2004

IT'S FOUR IN THE morning and I wake up, but it's not one of those interruptions where, after closing your eyes again, you immediately regain sleep. No. Not only are my eyes wide open, but my mind has started to play a movie that has yet to happen.

I never think about lack of sleep or insomnia, much less dreams or nightmares. If I wake up, I just deal with it. I can sleep tomorrow. But I'm mortified when I star in a story that I don't want to be a part of. At least not on the night before donating my sperm. So I try to manipulate the dream to lead it in the direction I choose—but is it a dream, or am I really awake?

Yesterday we toured La Jolla. We had lunch by the ocean, saw mansions and sunbathing sea lions. As usual, Gonzalo repeated one of his favorite phrases: "I could live here." We visited the Museum of Contemporary Art and entered a shop where we bought a tall, thin wood vase. It's a memento of the day we created the embryos. *The embryonic age. It will always be with us*, I thought.

In her most recent email, Karen wished me a wonderful Thanksgiving. She was hoping to see me during the donation—I didn't think that was going to happen—and assured me that everything was in order.

Dr. Wood's office confirms this: "We just saw your donor and she's reacted very well to the medications. She has between eight and ten follicles in formation. We'll check her again tomorrow. The retrieval will happen on Wednesday or Thursday."

I've calculated all the possibilities, trying not to leave anything to chance in my dramaturgy. Karen has been invaded by gonadotropins meant to stimulate the growth of her ovarian follicles. Apparently, these hormones are working. I don't think it'll be necessary to up the dosage this time. I imagine she's already received her last treatment, because in order for Dr. Wood to perform the retrieval, around thirty-six hours must have passed from her last injection.

As for the donation itself, the clinic will give Karen an intravenous sedative, and her eggs will be retrieved through a transvaginal puncture, monitored by an ultrasound. More specifically, Drs. Wood and Anderson, and their colleague Dr. Catharine Adams, will insert an ultrasound probe into the vagina, allowing them to see what they're doing. Through the vaginal wall they'll use a suctioning needle to reach the follicles and aspirate the eggs. By the time the eggs are retrieved from Karen's body, I will be ready with my sperm donation. Both she and I have been receiving oral antibiotics in preparation.

Mary, for her part, has already started treatment with Lupron. This medication will help ensure that her estradiol (a form of estrogen) is controlled and that her uterus lining is ready to facilitate the implantation of the embryos selected to be transferred to her womb.

Everything is carefully timed. We must be on the lookout for any calls from the doctor in the next twenty-four hours.

I'm asked to be at the clinic the next day at twelve noon.

Gonzalo, Esther María, and her husband, Néstor, come with me, but they remain downstairs in the mall. I'm wearing a red shirt, for good luck, and no cologne. Karen is already in the operating room. I give the nurse the catalog of Ana Mendieta's exhibition so that she can give it to Karen with a note: "I will always be grateful to you for helping me fulfill my dream of becoming a father."

Once again, I get ready to produce a sperm sample—this time the definitive one, the one that will help form my baby.

Afterward, I wait outside for a few minutes for Dr. Adams, who comes out to meet me with a serious expression. "This sample is not what we expected," she says.

I almost faint, but she asks me not to worry, says that my earlier sperm—the frozen ones they transferred from Los Angeles—can be used if it's not possible to obtain a better-quality sample. She asks me to go down to the cafeteria, have some tea, and, if possible, make another donation.

"Did you get to San Diego yesterday?" she asked. "We always recommend that fathers come two days earlier, rest the day before, and then leave their sample."

But no one had warned me about this, so I spent the previous day walking the streets of San Diego until I was so exhausted I couldn't feel my feet. I must have killed all my sperm.

"No, I'm not going down for tea," I reply. "I want to make the donation right now."

Thirty minutes later, like a robot, I produce another sample.

"This is fine! Now we'll get to work!" says the doctor, encouragingly.

"What do I do now? Where should I go? Who will find me?" I ask her.

"We'll notify you. Keep your phone on, because in twenty-four hours we'll know what to expect. Good news, though: thirteen eggs were retrieved."

It's no time to look back, but now that we're closer to meeting, even on a cellular level, I can't help but think that my daughter is a miracle. My miracle.

She doesn't have an official name yet; she's not even an embryo yet. For now, all we have are two cells waiting to unite. But she's already started to exist. She's already two weeks old, in fact. Because life began the moment the follicles developed.

So I feel as if my daughter already exists. The uncertainty is reduced because of Louise Joy, Natalie, Zoe, Alba, Adam, and Valentin, the miracle babies who pioneered the journey. You, my darling daughter, are going to harness the entirety of their experience as you develop.

The first test-tube baby, Louise Joy, was conceived in November 1977 and born on July 25, 1978, in England. At first, artificial insemination was just an experiment, but it ended up revolutionizing human conception, ushering in a new era. Louise Joy then had a sister, Natalie, also created in a lab. Five years after Louise Joy's birth, the magic continued: in Australia, Zoe became the first child born from a frozen embryo.

In Barcelona, a couple who feared that they would transmit hemophilia to their children decided to have a baby in vitro, and at the embryonic level, they selected the sex. Why did gender matter? Females can be *carriers* of hemophilia, but males have a higher chance of suffering from the disease. Seven embryos were analyzed, and doctors chose the one that would become a girl. Alba was born in 1997.

The evolution of assisted reproductive techniques has, in turn, brought new bioethical debates. Adam's birth in Colorado in 2000 marked the era of "designer babies," although others prefer the term "genetically modified babies." The idea was to conceive a child, Adam, who would be compatible with Molly, his sister. In this case, the girl, just six years old, suffered from

Fanconi anemia, a fatal disease. To survive, she needed a stem cell transplant from a compatible newborn. Adam was tailored to her needs using a donor's cytoplasm sample.

His creation would need to fulfill three premises: he couldn't have his sister's disease, he had to be compatible with her, and he had to be a viable embryo. Not all embryos become babies: as I had been told repeatedly, it's something that's "in God's hands." His birth was successful, and the lifesaving cells were obtained from his umbilical cord.

The savior baby, as some called him, was conceived and born to save a life. That birth involved stem cells; tomorrow it could be a kidney, or a lung. Would his parents see him as an experiment, as an organ bank, rather than a person in his own right? At birth, Adam was in fact confirmed as a savior, but what if he hadn't been able to provide the stem cells that Molly needed to survive?

Valentin was also born in 2000; the first French child conceived using preimplantation genetic diagnosis (PGD), he became the first eugenic baby. In Valentin's case, the parents sought genetic superiority not to save another child, as in Adam's case, but to make him perfect. It was a type of genetic correction.

Valentin's parents had already lost three children due to an enzyme deficiency in the liver. To prevent a recurrence, doctors extracted cells from the fertilized egg before implanting it in the mother's uterus, studying them to detect disease and implanting only "normal" embryos. This time, the child was born healthy.

Today any embryos that aren't transferred to a uterus can be cryopreserved at very low temperatures for later use. The intracytoplasmic sperm injection (ICSI) technique can also be used, in which a sperm chosen for its quality is introduced into the egg to increase the chances of fertilization. And to help the embryo implant itself in the uterus lining, it can be subjected to assisted hatching, which consists of piercing the protective covering of the embryo, almost always with an acid, to enable its implantation.

How will my daughter be born? I will soon know. At least I have at my disposal all of these techniques to bring her into the world. Now all I have to do is wait.

MY THIRTEEN BABIES

DECEMBER 2, 2004

IT'S SIX THIRTY IN the morning. Another long day lies ahead of us. We're waiting for a call from the clinic to see how many of the thirteen retrieved eggs have been fertilized. I don't want to stay in the room. While the others gradually wake up and get ready, I circle the hotel. It's a cold morning. By noon it will be hot. This is San Diego weather.

We have breakfast together in a café in La Jolla. Esther María, who has a weakness for dogs, bends over to pet a Labrador; it barks at her and nips her breast. We get scared: a dog bite!

Should we go to the ER? On reflection, we decide the bite is superficial. The owner of the animal is unfazed, ignoring our concern. The waiter asks if we need help.

"That's what you get for petting animals without asking for permission," I say with a brotherly lack of sympathy. "Either the dog was angry, or it fell in love with you. Who knows?"

We wander through a nursery and are amazed by the variety of plants. Gonzalo wants to take several samples home with him, but Néstor is right: most of those plants wouldn't survive in Miami's tropical climate.

I find it hard to remain in the moment. *By now, a sperm must have already pierced the cell membrane of each of the thirteen eggs. The two nuclei must have merged and each contributed its genetic endowment. The zygote is already on its way. Now we have to see how many zygotes will survive in a test tube.* Pulling myself back to my surroundings, I ask an employee about the "Dream Weaver" hosta I'm standing beside, thinking it might grow in Florida, but again my thoughts go elsewhere. *During that incubation period, the zygote begins to divide into two, three, and up to four cells.*

The nursery employee begins to explain how to take care of the hosta I asked about, but I interrupt him when I receive the first call of the day.

"All thirteen eggs were fertilized," the clinic tells me. "Now we must wait and see how many manage to survive until tomorrow." After fertilization, only about 70 percent usually survive—sometimes less. I'd be happy having six survive.

Now Mary has to be ready for the transfer, which will happen around eleven the next morning. I leave her a message. The moment has come.

I mentally block the lapse of time between when I receive the news and the next day at the clinic. In future years, nothing will come to mind when I try to recall those hours. It's a void. I'm lost in thought, I suppose.

We get to the clinic half an hour before the transfer. Everything is ready, but Mary hasn't arrived yet. Suham, the receptionist, tells me that they called her and left several messages. Once again, panic ensues.

"Where are you, Mary?" I shout in exasperation. Gonzalo tries to calm me down, telling me that there's no need for the added stress. He's right, of course—but the embryos can't wait for her. If she doesn't arrive on time, we'll have to cancel the transfer and cryopreserve the embryos. God knows how many would survive once thawed.

"I'll be there soon" is all Mary says when she finally calls me. In other words, she isn't in the building yet, or in the parking lot—maybe not even in La Jolla. I ask her to drive carefully; it's the only thing I can tell her at this point. Instead of coming with her partner and giving herself enough time to rest and relax before the embryos are placed in her womb, Mary is alone and running late, and I sense that she's flustered.

Dr. Adams comes out to the waiting room to greet me and hands me photos of the thirteen embryos. "Here are your babies."

"My children!" I exclaim. "How many are we going to transfer? Two, three, four, five . . . six?"

"I suggest three. It's my lucky number. I know you signed up to reduce the number of fetuses if this is a multiple pregnancy, but judging by the quality of these embryos, I can almost assure you that they're all going to be implanted," she replies.

Gonzalo and I take photos of ourselves holding up the Polaroid copies of the thirteen embryos.

Once back in a consulting room, I see Dr. Wood express his emotions for the first time. He's clearly very pleased with the results.

"With embryos like that," he says, "we're talking a 70 percent chance!"

Only 70 percent? It's as if he's thrown a glass of cold water in my face. I expected 100 percent!

Dr. Adams then shows me the three embryos she's selected. "These are the best," she says. "The remaining nine will be cryopreserved. We're going to discard only one, an embryo which isn't that great."

Discarded. An embryo that didn't fulfill the laws of nature. Was its division imperfect? Was the number of its cells not even?

Did it have more than one nucleus? Was it fragmented? Did it look like an oval instead of a sphere? Were the sperm stragglers embedded in its impenetrable zona pellucida? Who knows what problems it had? And who can guarantee that the remaining embryos, still at an early developmental stage, don't have some chromosomal aberration that will prevent them from evolving and transforming into fetuses? I already knew that not all embryos turn into babies. That's not in my hands, nor in the doctor's, nor in Mary's readied uterus.

Now Gonzalo and I have to decide whether we should be more aggressive and transfer more than three embryos or follow the doctor's advice. If we transfer six and they all implant, I'll have to be prepared for the doctor to inject potassium chloride into four of the fetuses' tiny hearts to stop their beating. In fact, even if three implant, I've already promised Mary I'll destroy one of them. My signature is etched on the contract. There's no turning back.

"And what are the chances that Mary will lose the pregnancy if we do a fetal reduction?"

The doctor explains that this isn't the issue. "The chances of losing it are slim," she says. "Five percent."

"Five? And who says that we won't be in that five percent?"

She ignores my question and continues with her explanation. "The problem is the emotional fatigue that fetal reduction entails. You think you can do it, but when the time comes to make that decision, it's very difficult, believe me."

And I do believe her. I'm already wondering how to tell Mary that I'm sorry, but I can't stick a needle in the tiny heart of one of my children. I'd have to flip a coin and decide whom to annihilate. It would be torture. The one on the right, the one in the center, the one on the left?

Perhaps the best decision now is to transfer only two embryos.

If both attach to the uterus, maybe Mary will be willing to carry the twins to term.

No, three. I *have* to transfer three. I *have* to be that aggressive. We're facing a fairly high percentage of probabilities, but it's 70 not 100 percent.

Done. Mary is taken to the operating room. She has to be relaxed, recalling pleasant moments. Clinic staff ask her to lie on her back, with her knees drawn up to her chest. The then doctor inserts a catheter with the three class A embryos of four cells each into her vagina, and passes them from the cervical canal to the carefully prepared uterus. After the transfer, she has to rest for a few hours. From there she'll be pushed in a wheelchair to her car and advised to stay in bed for two days, without getting up at all—even to go to the bathroom.

My three babies are already starting to grow in Mary's womb! They're beginning to divide into thousands of cells. Soon they'll turn into beautiful fetuses.

By the time Mary is up and out of bed, they'll already be two weeks and three days old.

DONUM VITAE

DECEMBER 4, 2004

THE TRANSFER WAS A success, I'm told. I figure that means there was no mishap, no bleeding. But there are no guarantees. There are never guarantees in assisted reproductive procedures.

As I pore over the photos of my thirteen babies, I can't help but visualize their fates. One, discarded; three inside Mary, waging a battle to survive; and nine, asleep on ice. They're class A, which makes them almost perfect—but in these processes *nothing* is perfect. Five of them were naturally fertilized—if we can call this natural—and eight were fertilized through intracytoplasmic sperm injection (ICSI). In other words, the first ones were achieved in vitro and the rest by means of ICSI. For that latter group, a needle seven times thinner than a hair was used to penetrate the cytoplasm of the egg and inseminate it.

The three embryos transferred to Mary's womb had four cells each, and one of them underwent assisted hatching to make its implant viable. Of the nine that were cryopreserved, seven are four-cell and the rest two.

———

THE FAMILY IS happy. My mom is excited about the idea of becoming a grandmother again in nine months. At my office, my
colleagues have followed each step of the retrieval process, the
transfer, and even both of my sperm donations, and they're eager
for news.

Amid my euphoria, I receive an email from Karen thanking
me for the catalog, wishing me luck and happy holidays, and
opening the door to keeping in touch.

I'll send her pictures of the baby when it's born. I'll try to
keep in touch with her without making her feel undue intrusion.
It's a relationship that, in the long run, could be beneficial for
the child.

Karen is not the mother, I know. The mother and/or father
is the one who *intends* to be so—who raises, educates, plays with,
and endures bad nights with their children. The rest are donors,
carriers, genetic code suppliers.

I'm committed to my remaining twelve babies. However, I
feel as if I've committed a sin with the one who was discarded:
Who decides what is or isn't a sin?

Where has my imperfect little baby gone? Limbo? To that
space between heaven and hell, that gray area where, for centuries,
children who died before being baptized were cast? Fortunately,
limbo no longer exists. The Catholic Church decided to abolish
it. For John Paul II, limbo was a theological hypothesis, not a
dogma. If we must all be saved, if that is one of God's premises,
then I feel calmer. In the end, what fault does an embryo, a newborn, a child have if its parents didn't get to baptize it?

That you, my imperfect one, existed at all is God's work. God
is the creator of life. God is on my side here. God isn't going to
abandon you. And the Church?

Infertility is a winnable battle, but assisted reproductive techniques have caused a real commotion in the Catholic Church.

Before being implanted, embryos are already human beings in the eyes of the Church. This was established by the Congregation for the Doctrine of the Faith (the arm of the Catholic Church tasked with clarifying doctrine) in the 1987 document *Donum Vitae*, which made an "urgent call to safeguard the values and rights of the human person in interventions on procreation." For the Congregation, an embryo obtained through an in vitro process is a human being and has the right to live—we're talking here about two, three, four, or eight cells, depending on their development. For others, the embryo gains humanity the moment it's implanted in the uterus lining. So at what point does it become a human being? With fertilization or implantation? With the first heartbeat, with the first brain signal? Or when it has developed and its birth is imminent?

The initial error that I find in *Donum Vitae* is that procreation is seen only through marriage—that between a woman and a man. It is assured in *Donum Vitae* that a child is the permanent sign of the traditional conjugal union. But that doesn't reflect reality. What about the children of single mothers who've been abandoned by their husbands? What happens if one of the parents dies of natural causes or an accident? What about men for whom marriage to a woman is unimaginable, yet who feel an undeniable drive toward fatherhood?

Concurrently, the Congregation considers that surrogacy is illicit, since it represents "an objective lack of the obligations of maternal love, conjugal fidelity, and responsible motherhood." Tell that to the thousands of intentional parents who are thrilled to undertake the obligations of parenthood due to the blessing of surrogacy.

The Congregation's opposition to medical intervention in

cases of infertility, even in marriages where one of the partners is sterile, is contradictory. If, for example, certain human beings have a fatal disease, will their fate be to resign themselves to their deterioration until their final days, or may they fight with the help of science? Diseases that two centuries ago were terminal today can be curable, thanks to technological and medical advances. Is it wise to abandon progress and follow the mandates of fate? If a couple is infertile, why can't they resort to new breeding techniques if, ultimately, the only creator is God?

A more recent instruction of a doctrinal nature, *Dignitas Personae* (2008)—also from the Congregation for the Doctrine of the Faith—aims to go even further by granting the human embryo, from the beginning, "the dignity proper to a person." Something that the Congregation didn't dare do in *Donum Vitae*, according to the new instruction, in order "to avoid a statement of an explicitly philosophical nature."

But how can a two-cell embryo be considered a person, if in *Dignitas Personae* itself it's noted that only a third of women who seek help in assisted reproduction end up with a baby? Not all embryos, it's known, develop into fetuses. Most don't even make it past the initial cell division stage. So, can a two-cell embryo be considered a person with rights?

To deny life through assisted reproductive techniques is to blind oneself to the reality constituted by more than a million test-tube babies who have come into this world. *Donum Vitae* states that "human life is sacred because from its beginning it involves 'God's creative action'"—divine action that is surely evident in *every* baby, including test-tube babies.

GONZALO AND I head over to visit our friend Marina at her New York apartment. She and her husband Alex have started looking for a baby.

"We do our homework every day," they tell us. Marina is forty years old. "We're so close. And you?"

"We've already done the transfer," I explain. "We should have news in fifteen days. Our children will be about the same age!"

The stepbrother of Tatiana, another friend, just had triplets in San Diego. The children arrived safely, but they were premature. The surrogate mother is now having health troubles. She had a complicated delivery and lost a lot of blood. Apparently, she'll have to undergo another operation, a hysterectomy. She won't be able to have any more children—not even her own.

THE THIRD ACCIDENT

DECEMBER 16, 2004

"MY BELLY FEELS HEAVY," Mary tells me. That's a good sign, I guess.

I think we're going to have at least one baby. Although we were excited about the possibility of having twins. God willing.

Mary feels good. She has the strange but not unpleasant sensation that something is growing inside her. Gonzalo and I are excited. Soon we will have to come up with a name. Although it's still too early, right? Is it bad luck to name a baby who hasn't been conceived yet? Actually, our babies *have been* conceived. Whether or not they've yet implanted themselves is another story.

Triplets? No. That would be too much. What happened to Tatiana's stepbrother's surrogate mother was horrible. I don't want any more accidents. I don't want anything to happen to the wonderful Mary either. In her own way, she seems excited. She's not very expressive, but I've gotten used to that.

On December 16 we're invited to a party to celebrate the eve of Saint Lazarus Day. A *cubanada*, as our friends from New York call it. Jorge and Hugo commemorate the day each year at their home in downtown Miami, surrounded by exotic plants and a mini-zoo with leopards, monkeys, crocodiles, and cockatoos. We attended one of those parties as newcomers from Cuba.

On December 16 we'll also find out if we'll be having one or two babies. At ten in the morning—one in the afternoon in Miami—Mary will get a blood test to detect whether or not she's pregnant.

IT'S TWO IN the afternoon. I'm heading to the kitchen to make a salad. I'm feeling pretty relaxed. Everyone in our circle is awaiting the news. My mom and sister have called me twice already. We're planning to announce the results to the rest of our friends that evening, at the feast of Saint Lazarus. It'll be a good celebration. I'll light a candle and ask the holy protector of health that my baby, or babies, develop well in Mary's womb. May they be born healthy and beautiful. I'll have to wear something purple to the party. It's Saint Lazarus's color.

I have yet to finish preparing the salad when I get the call from Angela at the clinic.

"Negative," she says, and we're separated by silence.

"Does that mean the test needs to be redone?" I ask, confused.

"I'm sorry. The doctor will talk to you next week to discuss the next step."

"Is there any room for error? And Mary . . . ?"

So we're in the 30 percent. We didn't make it to the successful 70. Wishful thinking.

Having heard me on the phone, Gonzalo walks in, sees my expression, and understands.

"Nothing?" He looks as devastated as I feel. "What happened? Didn't they say that those three embryos would stick?"

What can I tell him? They cheated us. Maybe Mary didn't do what she was supposed to do. Maybe we should change surrogate mothers. Start over, pass the test, be chosen, choose. More months and months of searching. Wait, what if it was the embryos? Perhaps my embryos all have chromosomal aberrations and will never develop into fetuses, much less babies. My remaining embryos, which haven't had a chance to become people, are orphans on ice. But they'll have a father—why not? They're class A; and four-cell embryos have a better chance of surviving the critical thawing time.

"What are you going to do?" Mary asks me when we finally speak.

The truth is I don't know. Now I have to once again think things through, make another decision. I can't stand having to make decisions. And I'll also have to call my mother and sister and be consoled, and it weakens me to be consoled. I can't bear to console or be consoled.

"Do you want to continue?" I ask Mary. She answers with the same question.

"I want my child; that's all I'm asking for," I reply.

But I expect more from Mary. I want her to say yes, that we *have* to continue, that this was a mere accident and nothing more. That next time it will work. That maybe we should be more aggressive and communicate to Dr. Adams that instead of three, we want to transfer four, six, or all of the embryos that we have left. I want to hear that Mary is committed to me, ready to sacrifice herself in search of my baby.

After speaking with the doctor, I'll call Mary again and we'll come to a decision. Everyone at the agencies already knows. Melinda and Becca offer their condolences as if I've lost a child: I've lost three of my "children-not-people."

My mom, when I muster the courage to call her, is struck by disbelief. My sister is shattered. I don't want to hear any more questions; I keep the conversations brief.

Jorge calls me to give me directions to the party, but I can't go; I can't face everyone and tell them about my failure. I have lost three of my babies. There will be no candles for Saint Lazarus. There will be no purple clothes.

Too much hope. "That kind of embryo sticks," everyone at the clinic had said. So it must've been Mary's fault. Perhaps her three-year-old daughter didn't let her rest, couldn't withstand her immobility.

Or maybe this is a sign that I'm not meant to be a father. I already tried with all my might. I feel like I've run out of energy.

Tatiana's stepbrother obtained the eggs from his first donor. The gestational mother became pregnant with the first transfer. All three embryos implanted themselves. Today he is the father of triplets. I, on the other hand, am part of the 30 percent.

I can't bear to be this depressed; I must leave this helpless state behind. A person can overcome anything. It was just another accident; but my nine other babies are still waiting, asleep in tubes stored at low temperatures; one of them will become a beautiful and healthy girl.

For a moment, I have no doubts. I remember that on the last night of 1999, I dreamed of you. And now I see you drawing nearer. This is another obstacle that I must and can overcome. Your undefined face in the dream helps me carry on. Don't disappear from my weak memory. Stay here.

Now we must be more pragmatic. No more melodrama. This time around, I won't even turn to Nina Simone. Gonzalo begins to clean up the house, then works in the garden. The time will come to speak, to reconstruct the script of possible errors. How did we not think of this one? Negative or positive. Two simple options.

I can't decipher whether the pain stems from failure or from loss.

While Gonzalo tackles weeds, I review our budget. The expenses have gone through the roof. The day my daughter arrives I'll be awash in debt. I need to know how high the figure will go, to what extent I can get into debt: everything has a limit.

With the lawyers, labs, medical consultations, Mary's preparation for the transfer, and the egg retrieval, we've spent $67,659.29. And we're not even halfway there yet.

But tomorrow's another day.

Gonzalo doesn't want us to have anyone over at the house. It's best if we watch a movie or read, he thinks. I decide that I need silence. And I realize that I'm ready for failure. What I'm not willing to do is lose my embryos, one by one. Three in one go. Maybe I should've been more cautious and transferred two, or maybe one. If Mary is the cause of these negative results, I sacrificed my babies.

It's late. I should go to sleep. Let time pass as quickly as possible.

Before we go to bed, Marina calls us. She's pregnant.

2005

THE ARRIVAL

NEW YEAR

JANUARY 2005

IF LIFE BEGINS FROM the moment the embryo is formed, I've already lost three children. Does life begin at birth, or when we're in the womb—or even earlier? I can't see their faces. I don't know if they ever existed, whether or not I should forget them.

I wonder if I should continue with Mary. I talk to Dr. Wood. He doesn't understand what could've happened. None of the three perfectly selected embryos managed to attach itself. I have two options, he says: try again with Mary or find another gestational mother.

"If you're not worried about money, you can try with another mother," says the doctor.

I'd like him to be more specific. I'd like him to tell me that my remaining embryos are viable, that Mary can definitely carry a pregnancy to term with one of my children. Of course I'm concerned about money—but precisely *because of* the money, I can't afford to lose all of my embryos.

"I don't think the problem was Mary," he asserts.

So who was it, doctor? You, the moon? My conversation with the doctor goes nowhere.

I check the database at the agency once more. There's Louise, mother of two children, married to a soldier. She's a first-time gestational mother. I can't bring myself to stop at any of those women's faces begging to be chosen. To do so would require an impetus that I no longer have, so I decide to continue with Mary.

We will try one more time.

"They called me from the clinic and were very tough on me," Mary says when I phone to tell her. "They asked me if I had rested enough, if I'd had sex."

Someone has to be strong with her; I can't do it. I have no right to claim anything from her. At least the clinic also has doubts. The doctors want to find the reason I fell into the terrible 30 percent.

From now on, I've decided to no longer speak to anyone about the process. It will be my secret. I will bear the burden of making all the decisions. I won't be able to cry or celebrate with anyone. That way I will avoid being comforted. If the pregnancy is confirmed, I will wait until Mary is twelve weeks along and only then will I break the news. To my family, my friends—even Gonzalo.

In order to continue with Mary, I must make additional bank transfers. I enter a state of terror with my finances. Two countdowns begin: the monetary one and the one with the viable embryos. If I have nine cryopreserved embryos, and if (as is usual) not all of them survive the thawing, I will have access to only another two attempts, should I decide to transfer three embryos at a time.

Now we must wait for Mary to menstruate. Then the doctor will evaluate her and give her the go-ahead to start a new cycle. We may be able to do it in February, whereupon my baby would be born in October or November. If we're blessed with twins, they would arrive in September, or perhaps earlier. I don't want to get my hopes up, but I still—despite everything—have a feeling that my daughter will be born this year. I close my eyes and feel her hug me and hide her face in my neck. We are one.

She already exists, although, for her, time is standing still. She can't grow. She's far away from me, sleeping. I can't read her stories at night; I can't even caress her in my dreams, sing to her, make up stories. I can't tell her to always remember that I'm her father, to not forget me, that I'll always be by her side.

She'll think that I've abandoned her forever in a sealed and labeled glass container, immersed in a tank of liquid nitrogen. Medical technology has stopped her metabolism, and she could live like that for years. Then I realize that eternal life exists: she is the proof.

My nine babies are two weeks and three days old. They've already been created; now I want them to wake up and begin to grow in Mary's womb—*that* is why I made them come into the world. I want to feel how, each month, one, two, or three of them are transformed as they develop in the womb. I will wait for them; eventually they will cry, and there will no longer be anyone to stop their metabolism, because life will have begun.

I ask everyone around me—Gonzalo included—not to inquire about the process's status. It's not superstition—or maybe it is. It's not wariness either—at least, I don't think so. It's simply an attempt to protect myself. From now on, I will bear the burden of making all the decisions. I want to feel in control, avoid comfort and consolation, forget failures. We will all celebrate together in due course. I will share only the successes, not the failures. Disappointment is carried in private, not in a collective act that magnifies it. I've told them only that I'm going to continue with Mary, and that I will not stop until my daughter is a reality. When? They'll soon find out.

Not a night goes by without me thinking about my babies.

Marina tells us that she now knows the gender of their baby: they're expecting a girl. Her name will be Luna.

MY THREE BABIES

Mary doesn't feel comfortable in her neighborhood and has decided to move. A convicted sex offender, recently released from prison, has moved into her apartment complex.

"I spoke about this problem with the building's owner," she tells me, "but he said that the man had already served his sentence for society; that he was found guilty and already paid for his crime."

She is upset, worried about her daughter. Although she never leaves the youngster alone or allows her to play in the hallways, the man's presence is a latent danger. She takes her daughter to soccer practice four times a week and to riding lessons once a week. She's afraid to run into the man, who likely doesn't have a job. After all, Mary thinks, if he just got out of prison, who's going to give him work?

"The law shouldn't allow him to live in a building with children," she says. Mary doesn't know what specific crime he committed: if he abused girls, if he exposed himself, if he raped someone, if someone died at his hands. The only thing that's clear to her is that he's a registered sex offender.

I worry about her being stressed. Her estradiol is steady and she's menstruated twice, so her cycle is regular. Now it all comes down to her and to the availability of Dr. Wood to perform a new transfer. The embryos are ready to thaw and, if it were up to me, the sooner the better.

Mary's mother, a recently retired nurse, is leaving her rental condo in San Diego to move to Palm Springs with her Colombian boyfriend. Mary is thinking of moving to that apartment. Her younger sister doesn't want to go with her mother; she refuses to live in the desert. Mary suggests that they live together in the apartment and she'll pay her mother's rent. It's an excellent idea: Mary wouldn't be alone, her sister could help with her daughter, and it would be easier for Mary to rest after the embryo transfer.

I receive an email from Angela at the clinic.

"We just saw Mary and her ultrasound was perfect. We'll start with the Lupron next week, and if all goes well, we'll transfer the embryos on March 3."

Dr. Adams, when I speak with her, insists that more than three embryos would be risky.

"For an embryo to implant itself, one part has to do with the embryo itself, another with the preparation of the uterus, and a third with the transfer. There are too many factors. If any of them fails—and sometimes it has nothing to do with the uterus or the embryo—you'd lose the possibility of doing another cycle," she explains.

Mary keeps insisting that two is the maximum she's willing to carry. It's understandable. Dr. Wood, in turn, advises me that if I want two babies, I should use three embryos, but if I want only one, he recommends transferring two. Last time I transferred three and none developed.

Meanwhile, Mary is going to move before starting the treatment. This is good news.

In Miami, we continue remodeling the house. We decide to change the flooring. The current slabs are rustic; they will be a problem when the baby starts to crawl. Wooden floors would be best.

Your room is almost ready, my dear daughter. Still unfurnished, with just a small white closet. Knowing that we'll need a rocking chair to cradle you, we put one in place. But until Mary is pregnant and the baby's arrival is imminent, we won't buy a crib. And we'll assemble it only once you come home. It's family tradition.

I finally decide that three is the right number. I must follow the experts' recommendation. As much as I would like to transfer all nine embryos, if the level of preparation of the uterus isn't sufficient, I could lose them all. And that would truly be a crisis. I don't think I could start looking for an egg donor again.

Now I just want to sleep for weeks, for time to evaporate. For March 3, and then March 16, and then April 1 to arrive. But I must be patient. There's nothing I can do. This time I don't have to donate sperm, so I don't need to be relaxed. It all comes down to Mary, and whether the three chosen babies decide to wake up and survive their ice age.

They will be selected at random and transferred from the test tube into Mary, where an even longer captivity will commence: around thirty-eight weeks.

THE LULLABY

No one usually wakes up and thinks that today will be the day their life could change. At least I try to avoid that. I'm thousands of miles away from where my nine embryos sleep, and in a few hours the doctors will wake three of them up. I'm going to stay in Miami. I want Mary to be alone for the embryo transfer; I understand that my presence intimidates her.

I walk around the house awhile, go back to bed—what to do to make time pass? I think about calling Mary to find out how she feels before her trip to the clinic, but I realize it's better not to. I review some articles that I've been wanting to read.

I'm about to call Mary, despite knowing that I shouldn't. I just saw that it has started to rain in San Diego, and the weather forecaster says it will rain all day. What kind of sign could this be—good or bad? I don't want to return to the list of possible errors. I don't need to, because I'm confident that nothing else can happen to me. I will become a father this year. That's all I know.

I put my phone down again, unused, and imagine what Mary's

morning will be like, in her time zone three hours behind me. Mary will get up early, get ready, and after breakfast comb her daughter's lush hair. With a three-year-old girl, her life is busy. As Mary does every morning, she'll spend time with her; they'll play, they'll talk.

I know from earlier conversations that her mother has come from Palm Springs to take care of the child while Mary is in the clinic and during the required two days of bed rest. Her daughter's father will accompany Mary to the clinic.

They've already thawed the three embryos, which survived the risky event. Sometimes crystallization, due to the low temperature, destroys them. Mary has arrived and is relaxed, I'm told.

Eventually I'm informed that the transfer has been a success. I don't believe in success. Nobody tells me what percentage I will fall into now, nor do I want to know.

Dr. Wood calls me and recommends that Mary stay at the hotel closest to the clinic. They will make the arrangements and wheel her over.

"It's raining too much. What she needs is rest. The road can be very dangerous."

Though I want to talk with Mary and see how she's feeling, I decide to leave her alone. I won't call her. I'll let her sleep, rest, not dream. At least no nightmares.

And now it's time to wait for fifteen agonizing days to pass. I try to remember nursery rhymes—I must know some—but it seems I've forgotten them all. I can recall only the sad boleros that my grandparents used to sing me to sleep with. *He tied the naked bones with ribbons, crowned the dead skull with flowers, covered the horrible mouth with kisses and told her with a smile about his love.*

Oh God, what song will I sing to my child? It certainly won't be "Bodas negras." She's already in Mary's womb; she's already begun to develop. I can begin to think about my daughter now that she exists outside of a test tube, now that the low temperatures of the nitrogen tank have been left behind.

She's back in the real world, where by now she must have already divided into thousands and thousands of cells, impossible to count. And I don't know a single lullaby! I should start singing to her right now. Every night I will whisper to her until she falls asleep, so she feels that I'm by her side. And every day, when I wake up, the first thing I'm going to do is think about her.

I know she will hear me, because we've been connected since the day I dreamed of her, the last night of the previous century. I will feel her grow, I will see her cling to Mary's womb, and she will fight, because I know she also longs to meet me. She's not one to give up. She has been asleep on ice for three months, waiting for a prince charming, and her time has come.

She will hear my voice and recognize me, because from thousands of miles away I will say to her in a whisper: "Good evening—it's me, your dad, the one who has spent years searching for you and who won't rest until he has you in his arms, until he hugs you and gives you a kiss." As of today, my daughter is no longer a dream: she is my reality.

Duérmete mi niña, duérmete mi amor, duérmete pedazo, de mi corazón.＊

＊ *Hush-a-bye my little girl, hush-a-bye my love, hush-a-bye to you, the very piece of my heart.*

PREGNANT

MARCH 18, 2005

L IFE TRANSPIRES IN CIRCLES. Each child who comes into the world closes one loop and opens another that, in turn, must be closed. Then, in that infinite cycle, another circle appears, which someone else will seal. It's an endless chain, and children are its links. Sometimes you resign yourself to living with missing links, but the void remains all the same.

I just built my link. I've sculpted it piecemeal, and in a few months, I will be able to make the announcement. Until now, that hope has been my secret.

Today Gonzalo and I are hosting a family dinner at home. Everyone will be there, and I won't remind them that today also marks fifteen days since the transfer, that three links are maturing in Mary's womb. The clinic could call me in the middle of dinner with an update, but I wouldn't be able to scream with joy. Maybe my face would give me away; maybe amid the commotion I wouldn't hear the phone and they'd leave a message, and I'd lock myself in my room when I notice and listen repeatedly to the only word I want to hear: "positive." Then, I'd go back to our dinner, smiling, happy with my secret, which I would still need to keep for another two months.

My cousin Iliana, who wants to become a grandmother, is coming today, as well as my mother, sister, nephew, and cousins Romy and Betsy. We'll all be there, and someone will surely ask: How is Mary? What happened to the transfer? Is there a baby on the way? As is my new habit, I'll close down that line of conversation: no news yet.

While Gonzalo cleans the house, I return to Nina Simone. I'm not depressed; I just need to isolate myself and stop thinking until the call comes and delivers the magic word, the only one the clinic can utter, because *this* time I will be among the percentage of those who succeed. *I would give anything, anything I own, if you'd be my love. What more, what more can I say?* I know it will be good news. I'm sure of it, because during these fifteen days I have sung to my baby every night, and every day before getting up I have said good morning. Nina brings me good luck; she comforts me. She is my consolation.

Gonzalo and I head to the market in preparation for our dinner guests. When we get to the parking lot, I get a call.

"Congratulations, Dad," whispers Mary's sweet voice, which I can barely hear. I don't react; I remain silent so that she'll repeat the news, so that she'll say the word I've been waiting for. With the first transfer I was told "negative" and now I want to hear "positive," but Mary doesn't use technical terms; she congratulates me again and adds, "I'm pregnant!"

I'm speechless. I want to cry, laugh, but I do neither. I manage only to say, "Thank you . . ."

What more can I say?

Angela calls from the clinic a moment later. Mary hasn't had any symptoms yet. No dizziness, no nausea, and best of all, no pain in the lower abdomen or spotting. Angela explains that the blood test showed a human chorionic gonadotropin (hCG) level of 120. If it had been below 30, the pregnancy would've been considered negative. This essential hormone is produced by the embryo when it implants itself into the uterine lining, and later by the placenta. Tomorrow the clinic will repeat the test and, to confirm the pregnancy, the hormone should have doubled. One of hCG's functions is to maintain the production of progesterone until the placenta takes over that job. In the absence of sufficient progesterone, menstruation begins. For the first three months, therefore, Mary—as a surrogate mother—will have to take a daily supplemental dose of progesterone.

At dinner, my cousin Romy mentions that she's ready to have a baby.

Iliana, her mother, is counting down the days to become a grandmother. "I want a granddaughter, if you can manage it, Romy," she says with a smile.

Then Iliana turns to me. "I think you're going to have a girl too. Look at your dad: he makes more women than men."

True, my father had a boy and five girls; one died a few months after birth.

I try to change the subject, but my mom brings it up again.

"What if they're twins? How would you handle that?"

We would figure it out. The thought of having two babies thrills me. It's better to be prepared than surprised. I say nothing.

It's FRIDAY AND Mary is up early to repeat the blood test that will determine whether the hormone has doubled.

"I'm sorry. The number isn't what we expected. It went up to only 187," they tell me from the clinic. "We're going to repeat the exam on Monday, and if the number hasn't gone up quite a bit, we'll stop the estrogen dose and wait for Mary to menstruate again."

They give me no other explanation. It's as simple as that: the number isn't what they expected. They're direct, to the point; they don't soften the blow. Instead of the 240 we were hoping for, we got to only a pitiful 187. Not only is there no chance of having twins—they would've spiked the hCG—but it's highly probable that I won't become a father this time either.

Mary can't be blamed. It all depends on the embryo and its chromosomal quality. If there's any error, it will detach itself. Nature is wise.

Another three babies thrown into the abyss. Will any survive?

I count the minutes, the hours. I live in a constant battle against time. Another eternal weekend.

ATTACHED

APRIL 1, 2005

"IF YOU DON'T HURRY, you're going to be grandparents instead of parents," my friend Cristina jokes. Those are the sorts of conversations that I prefer to ignore or try to forget.

Of course this is something that worries me. I haven't let time pass because I want to enjoy myself. I haven't stopped the arrival of my baby to take a vacation in Europe. If she hasn't arrived, it's because God hasn't put her in my path.

My mom had me at twenty. I grew up with a mother who was younger than the rest of my classmates' moms, and she's always been my pride. She was young, she was a college student, but she became a professional. My grandmother took care of everyday life, and my mother dealt with its essence: going to school meetings, taking me to doctor appointments, discussing my career choices. She and my grandmother were the necessary balance in my life. I want to be there for my baby in its everyday life and its essence. Gonzalo will help make the formula work, but my age betrays me.

You already know, my little one, that you've been a desired girl since before I dreamed of you. You will not interrupt my youth. You will not limit my outings, my vacations, my relationships with my friends, my professional promotions. You are the priority. You will be my daughter, my friend, my outings, my vacations, my profession. But I won't be twenty when you're born, and it terrifies me to think that, when you reach my age, I may no longer be by your side. So I resolve to enjoy every minute with you.

I start to calculate how old I'll be at each stage of your life, and I become dejected. A twenty-year-old dad is an absent dad. A forty-year-old dad is a present dad, but for a shorter period of time. There are pros and cons that must be weighed—but I have no choice. This is how it will be and we'll have to adjust. When you turn fifteen, I'll be sixty-one.

Can you imagine? And things will get even worse. When you're thirty, I'll be an old man of seventy-six, already retired. At forty, you'll have an old man of eighty-six as a father, if health is on my side. And that's where I stop counting. That train of thought makes no sense. I have to care for my own health like I care for you.

The good thing about my having had a young mother is that now you will enjoy a vibrant grandmother. Everything has its reward. That's why you must be born as soon as possible. This is your year, our year. So please hold on to Mary's uterus lining. Fight with all your strength; I'm here, waiting with open arms.

IT'S CLOSE TO midnight, so it's time to go to bed. As I do every day, I'm going to sing to you so that you can sleep peacefully.

I wake up the next day, Monday, and think of you. Mary calls hours later and lets me know that they've already taken her blood sample and that the clinic will call me with the results. Sometimes hCG takes seventy-two hours to double instead of forty-eight;

I've been told this repeatedly. Sometimes two embryos are implanted and the third begins a countdown. Although one sends signs of life, the other diminishes the energy that the placenta and brain synthesize.

"Congratulations, the pregnancy is confirmed," the doctor tells me.

I can't believe it.

"And the number?"

"Five hundred and fifty-nine."

"How high should it be tomorrow?" I ask, happy and anxious.

"No further tests are needed. This is proof that there's a developing embryo."

"That will become a fetus?"

"We won't know until we detect the heartbeat through a transvaginal ultrasound in two weeks. Sometimes there's an amniotic sac, but the zygote doesn't evolve," explains the doctor.

I'll have another fourteen days of waiting. My life now transpires in two-week spans. But tonight I'll be able to sleep peacefully and my daughter, from afar, will surely sense my lullaby even stronger. Because she's growing, and I know that she's already begun to live. Otherwise, why would I be filled with such hope?

HEARTBEATS

APRIL 18, 2005

I'M WAITING FOR MARY to pick me up outside the San Diego train station. We're going to her ultrasound appointment together for proof that you exist, that there's a developing heart and not an empty sac sending out misleading signals.

Mary is glowing. Her smile comforts me. Her tenderness gives me confidence. If we detect a heartbeat today, she'll begin to receive her fee, distributed in monthly payments.

She has started to feel nauseous in the morning. A good sign that hCG is rising and doing its thing. At short intervals, she interrupts the conversation and drinks water from a huge bottle.

"I have to drink almost a liter before I get to the clinic," she explains. They've recommended that she have a full bladder.

Her body has started to show signs of transformation, she tells me. She is constantly drowsy, is more sensitive to smells, and has breast tenderness. She expresses all this as a complaint and I reply that I'm sorry, although in reality I also celebrate the symptoms. She's pregnant. No doubt. We *will* find a beating heart inside the sac.

"I'm going to leave my daughter's father," she reveals. I'm not good at this sort of situation; I don't know how to comfort, so I oscillate between "What a shame!" and "Your girl must be so big . . ." The car is full of dolls, drawings, colored pencils. From what I can tell, her daughter is the center of everything. Luckily, Mary's younger sister is there to help, and I hope she'll continue to do so as the pregnancy progresses. She doesn't talk much about her mother, and I don't ask. All I know is that she was present during the embryo transfer, and I imagine she'll also be there when Mary goes into labor.

I would like to see where Mary lives, what her apartment is like, her daughter's room. But I've never been invited, and I refrain from the suggestion. Once, I mentioned that I wanted to drop off a gift and she asked that I leave it at her door. I insisted a little, and only managed to get her to pick it up from the parking lot. I couldn't even get to the front door.

I understand that she wants to protect her privacy, that she doesn't want to be evaluated. That she's against the idea of having an intruder come and question whether her house is neat or messy, comfortable or inadequate. I would actually never make such judgments; I'm just curious to see the environment in which my embryos will grow.

In the clinic's waiting room, there's always someone waiting with an expression of terror. Today it's a young couple. I'm eager to know their story, what level of infertility and despair they carry. They look at Mary and me as if we were a couple too, and the first thing they do is eye Mary's abdomen to try to detect if she's pregnant. It's not yet noticeable; no one could tell by looking at her alone—only at *us*, since we're radiating happiness. I'd love to know who they are, if they're going to try in vitro treatment, or if they'll hire an agency to find a gestational mother. I'd like to tell them about my experience, recommend Surrogate Alternatives, give them advice.

A staff member calls Mary first and I remain in the waiting room, next to the desperate couple. They don't talk to each other. Perhaps the husband doesn't want to spend another penny to make his wife, who's obsessed with having a child, happy. Maybe he has children from a previous marriage. With that attitude, the process will become even more difficult.

Mary is ready for the ultrasound when I'm called back. The room is so small that I barely fit next to her. She already has her legs raised and is waiting for the doctor to insert into her vagina the transducer, a type of white tube, covered with a sterile lubricant. Since the pregnancy is in its early stages, a transabdominal ultrasound wouldn't be able to detect the heartbeat.

Although there are no documented cases, I panic at the idea that the test could harm my embryos or cause a miscarriage. I know that ultrasounds don't use ionizing rays; they use acoustic waves. The frequency they transmit is imperceptible to humans.

Wouldn't it be better to wait for the embryo (or embryos) to be formed, though—for the fetus to throb and grow to a point where no sound wave could affect it? But I must trust strangers. I have no other choice.

"I can see two sacs—one larger, one smaller," the doctor says. "See there? If we can detect a fetal heartbeat at seven weeks— which is roughly where we are now, including the time before implantation—there's a high chance that the pregnancy is viable. Let's see what I find here. Look, do you see this?" he asks.

I certainly don't see anything! What appears on the small black-and-white monitor looks to me like abstract masses in motion. Mary is smiling, so I guess *she* sees something different.

"Can't you see how it beats?" he asks, seeing me squint. "I want to make sure we *all* see it."

I focus intently until I see a tiny dot that moves rhythmically. Apparently, that's the heart that we've been seeking.

The doctor then goes to the other embryo's sac, but there's no movement there.

"I don't think this one is viable. It isn't developed like the other one," he cautions, but adds that he's not sure. So I have at least one, maybe two living children inside Mary.

The doctor prints the image of the more developed baby's heart and gives me a photo. At last I have something tangible. I have a picture of my daughter. (The gender isn't apparent yet, of course, but ever since that long-ago dream, I've assumed my baby will be a girl.)

Hope surges in me. "In this case, the chances of having a baby are about 99 percent, right?" I venture. Because I know that someone always falls in that remaining 1 percent. Nothing is 100 percent safe in assisted reproduction.

"Things looks very good," the doctor replies, "although, indeed, anything can happen in a pregnancy. Your baby—we'll assume for now it's just one—is about seven weeks old, and her due date should fall on November 22."

What? That's just what I need. My daughter will be born on my pathetic stepfather's birthday, a man whom I've all but forgotten. We're going to have to move that date up or, better yet, delay it. And she'll be a Scorpio, like him. Ironies of fate. I've always thought that my stepfather fit the stereotype of a bitter Scorpio, and now my daughter is going to be born under that same sign. I decide to convince myself that he was an astrological mistake, and that I'm going to have a wonderful daughter, through whom I will learn to love Scorpios.

I don't want to hear anything else. I have up to two children, one of whom has a heart that's pumping at full speed.

Upon leaving, the receptionist congratulates me. "You're having twins!"

Oh God, out loud it intimidates me, even though I know it's still only a hypothetical.

Mary and I hug when we hear the word "twins." After so many attempts and failures, we leave the clinic with something concrete: the first photo of my child.

I BOARD THE plane and settle into my seat. As we're about to take off, a call comes in from my cousin Romy.

"Surprise! I'm pregnant! We just heard the heartbeat. She's due on the same day as my mother's birthday, November 30."

I can't afford to celebrate with her. I congratulate her and remind myself to keep my secret for two more months. I'm going to be a dad.

THE FOURTH ACCIDENT

MAY 2, 2005

MARY SENDS ME PHOTOS of the eight-week ultrasound. The lead embryo is getting stronger and stronger, she says, and at last the heartbeat has appeared in the second sac. There's hope for the smaller one, then. The doctor, however, is still pessimistic. He says that it looks weak, that he doesn't think it will develop.

But is there any chance? Possibilities always exist, he says. In another two weeks, the next ultrasound will give us a better idea as to whether the littler embryo will survive.

The ultrasound photo that Mary sent clearly shows both sacs, so I won't give up yet. They can be clearly distinguished. Inside each sac, a small seedlike image can be seen. Will they be two females, two males, one of each, or a solo female or male? Despite my longstanding assumption that I'll have a daughter, I don't actually have a preference. At first, Gonzalo and I were afraid of having a girl. What would we do when we had to take her to a public bathroom? While she's a toddler it won't be an issue; it gets complicated as girls grow, though: the obsession with pink, the princesses . . . But whoever God sends our way will be welcome.

The same day that I'm due to receive the results of the ten-week ultrasound, which will define the lives of my two children, I have to travel to the Bahamas. My editor is sending me to interview Shakira, who is releasing an album after four years away from the recording studio and has requested that I be the one to interview her, in person. I can't say no, yet neither can I let anyone know that I'm waiting for an important call and won't be able to focus. Since I've kept everything a secret, I can't give people any excuses—least of all Ceci, Shakira's representative.

It's my first trip to the Bahamas where Shakira is living and does much of her recording. The plan for the day includes visiting the studio, spending time with Shakira, seeing a recording rehearsal, and then taking a plane back to Miami.

When I arrive at the airport, I realize that my phone has no bars. I'll try to call the clinic from a public phone later on.

The band and the project team are staying at a hotel that overlooks the sea. It's a kind of multistory log cabin. Ceci is waiting for me. We sit on the terrace and talk about the album, about Shakira's tireless hours in the studio, and about the album cover, which she wants to show me exclusively.

"No one else has seen it. It's a big surprise," she says, revealing it to me.

I'm dumbfounded. The photo shows an angelic Shakira, a Renaissance Madonna, ecstatic, holding a naked baby in her arms. Is this the sign I'm looking for? Could Ceci have seen my worried face? Does Shakira want to send a message through the five-month-old baby she holds in her arms—her little cousin Luciana—that she's ready to be a mother?

We head over to the legendary Compass Point Studios, where Shakira is waiting for me. She has changed a lot since the last time I interviewed her; she's like another person. She has freed herself from countless layers of makeup, from her hair extensions. I'm in front of an all-natural Shakira. She's thrilled about the album: we talk about the cover, which has surprised me, about her relationship with her boyfriend, and I ask her outright if she wants to get pregnant, if having a baby is in her plans.

"It's the biggest project of my life. However, before that great project, I have a debt to myself, and it's a sabbatical year. Before I bring a child into the world, all I really want to do is scratch my belly for a while."

In other words, she's not pregnant. She's still young and on her honeymoon with her boyfriend. A long and intense tour comes next. The album, *Oral Fixation*, harmonizes well with motherly Shakira.

"I wanted to refer to a universal mother, the mother who feeds, gives, protects. I thought it was a lovely concept and the title needed an image, an anchor."

We finish the interview and she insists that I stay until the next day and accompany her to a recording. But it's not possible. I don't know how to explain that I must return in a few hours, that I can't spend another minute in the Bahamas; so I simply decline. Instead, we go immediately to the recording studio, where she ties her hair up with her scarf and dedicates my favorite song from the album to me. *No se puede morir con tanto veneno. No se puede dedicar el alma a acumular intentos. Pesa más la rabia que el cemento.* Shakira sings as if her throat were being ripped open, and she stretches her vowels with such power that it's almost impossible to believe that the resulting sound is all flowing out of her petite body.

Late in the day, I finally reach out to the clinic from an airport pay phone. The minutes pass as I wait on hold to speak

---

* "You can't die with such poison. You can't devote your soul to accumulating intentions. Fury weighs more than cement."

with the doctor. Each time someone at the clinic has put me on hold and I've had to wait for some explanation from the doctor, it's been bad news. I know the drill. So why am I in the Bahamas? My editor could have sent another writer, or we could have changed the date. Shakira would have understood. But no: it had to be that day; otherwise it would have been impossible to get her. Shakira was going to appear on one of our magazine covers, and we couldn't miss the opportunity to interview her.

"One of the embryos died," the doctor says. Then silence. Why doesn't he keep going? Does he want to hear me cry? "Mary's body gradually will absorb the sac until it disappears, and this process won't affect the other placenta. The other baby is growing, and its heart rate is strong. I'm sorry, I'm so sorry . . ."

And there I am, at the airport on a Caribbean island, unable to call anyone, without Nina Simone, with a three-hour wait before my flight leaves. I feel as if my skin is going to explode, like I'm intoxicated, covered with hives. I haven't eaten anything in quite a while; I've had only bottled water.

I've lost my child and I can't vent. I'm in an unknown place, surrounded by strangers who don't know, who cannot understand, that I've lost one of my babies.

It terrifies me to think that the death of one could damage the development of the other. The doctor said it wouldn't. Should I believe him? And what will happen to that empty sac—will it really disappear as promised?

With no other option, I begin to quietly pray, not so much to God as to my little one. *Don't leave me. I will sing to you before I go to bed tonight; when I get up, I will think of you. Stay with me. You're already a part of me. You're a piece of me. We can never part again.*

My daughter will have no siblings. She will grow up alone. She will be the daughter of old men. I tried for a sibling and had been delighted to know that Mary was carrying two babies in her womb. Had I been asking for too much? Shouldn't I consider myself lucky because I'm going to have at least one?

In the search, I've lost five children so far. Right now, I wouldn't know where they've gone, but I know that my daughter *will* be born and my sorrow *will* be alleviated the day I hold her in my arms.

There are still six frozen embryos. Who knows whether later, after having my daughter, I'll have the strength to start this insane process all over again? Maybe I'll wait for her to say, "I want a baby brother." Some years will need to pass, in any case. I'll need to be patient.

We will meet in November. I count the hours, the days. Meanwhile, I will continue to sing, from a distance, so that my baby falls asleep. Someday I'll let my daughter know that at least I tried.

THE FIRST IMAGE

"THIS IS ONE GORGEOUS baby!" exclaims Dr. Wood as he moves the transducer inside Mary. I can clearly see you on the monitor. Now you have a shape; you're no longer a tiny particle lost in a sac.

"Here's the head, the body, the arms, the legs. A complete baby." He pauses, looks at me, and smiles. Mary looks for my reaction, but I'm busy recording the scene. Today is the day that everyone will learn that you exist.

"Let's see if the baby wants to wake up," Dr. Wood says. He nudges Mary's abdomen, looks for a reaction from the baby, but the child is peacefully sleeping in a cradle of amniotic fluid, lifting one arm to settle back into a comfortable fetal position.

Today is Mary's last visit to the clinic. Her trips to La Jolla are over. Goodbye, Dr. Wood; goodbye, Dr. Adams. Now we have to face the real world.

An obstetrician-gynecologist in San Diego will see Mary, do her ultrasounds. It will be someone who's used to caring for surrogate mothers. There will be no surprises, and I won't have to explain our unusual situation.

The clinic prints and gives me a photo on which, for the first time, I can see that my daughter is more than an embryo. As of today, she is officially a fetus, the size of a lemon, about two and a half inches long. The fingers and toes have finished separating, so the previous amphibian image has disappeared. The nails have started to develop. When she's awake, she's doesn't stop moving. Her skeleton is already formed, but she still has extreme flexibility. The sac has become a full-blown placenta now, and her heart is pumping so hard it can already be heard on the ultrasound. She's "eating" well, but doesn't weigh even an ounce yet. She's so small.

The first trimester is about to end, so the risks of losing her have been greatly reduced. It's time to name her, because she's already a reality.

In the taxi, on the way to the airport, I call my mom.

"Mary is pregnant. We're going to have a baby. She's due in November. There were going to be two, but one died . . ."

I can't go on; I start crying uncontrollably. The cab driver looks at me sadly, as if a dear family member had died. Someone called him from the clinic on my behalf, so maybe he's used to picking up patients who are unhinged because a pregnancy isn't progressing or because an in vitro process has failed.

I can't tell my mom that my littlest baby struggled in Mary's womb to survive, tried to attach itself with all its might for weeks, even had a beating heart, but it couldn't survive. It was very weak and succumbed. I had already come to believe that there would be two of them, that my daughter would have a little brother. It was likely a boy. Male embryos are weaker and also heavier, I've been told. They say that in vitro fertilization produces more females than males. Women have one less chromosome.

You will be a girl. I know it; I'm convinced. But to confirm it, we'll have to wait for the sixteen-week ultrasound.

After I compose myself, I call Gonzalo, who is thrilled, but he already assumed the pregnancy was a go.

"I knew it," he exclaims. "I was waiting for you to call me with the news any minute now. I just knew this trip to San Diego was final. We have to start thinking about names."

I'm guessing that while I'm in the air on my way to Miami, Gonzalo will share the news with everyone. His parents will know in Cuba, his sister in Brazil, his other sister in Italy, Esther María in Los Angeles.

It's official: we're going to be dads. Well, we have been since we created the embryos. Since before they were kept at low temperatures to paralyze their metabolism. There's no turning back. Our daughter will be born this year. She will come into our lives, and in that instant, everything will change. We will not be the same.

On the return flight I begin to imagine her eyes, her face, her lips. They're still abstract. My abstraction. She will soon have a name. Choosing one will be the first thing Gonzalo and I do when I get to Miami.

Mary, sounding concerned, calls to let me know that her health insurance isn't active. The surrogacy agency told me earlier that it had been approved, and my understanding was that Mary had to pay for it because it was in her name, and then the agency would refund her the money. There's been a communication error from Surrogate Alternatives; they failed to tell me I was directly responsible for that payment, even though all the accounts were settled through the agency.

Conclusion? Mary has no insurance. We've run out of medical coverage.

But this is no time for bad news. I have a living baby growing inside Mary, a baby who will be born in six months.

IT'S A GIRL!

JULY 8, 2005

I T'S EASY TO FEEL paranoid if a stranger is carrying your child in her womb. Even more so if you don't know her house, her family, where she works, or how she thinks. A legal document is your only protection. There is no guarantee. As I've said before, nothing is 100 percent safe in assisted reproduction, and even less so in surrogacy. My baby is growing in an unknown body. That's my dilemma.

I'm not worried about what Mary eats, whether she leads a healthy life, whether she takes care of my baby as she would take care of her own. I trust her; I have no choice. And until now, it's always been clear in our conversations that the baby belongs to me, has always been and will always be mine; but it seems that the hormones are starting to do their thing, I can feel it. It's as if Mary were creating a shield and pulling away, forcing me to keep my distance. She's in San Diego, and I'm on the other side of the country. We're joined only by a phone that she rarely answers.

Why does she disappear like this? Doesn't she realize that I could lose my mind? She goes to the doctor, she gets tested for any fetal abnormalities, and she can't find the time to dial my number, talk to me or just leave me a message, or email me? Excuses are prolific: she lost the internet; her computer modem was damaged; her daughter threw the phone into the toilet.

Left without reassurance from Mary, I rack my brain trying to organize my desperate script of possible problems with the baby. Let's see, a blood test could tell us if the baby is developing well. There are genetic diseases that can be detected now with blood tests and other simple exams, as well as tests that are a bit more invasive, such as extracting a sample from the placenta (chorionic villus sampling) or from the amniotic fluid (amniocentesis).

Given that Karen donated her eggs at twenty-two and Mary is twenty-four, I don't think amniocentesis will be needed. It could put the pregnancy at risk, and that's the last thing we want right now. Just thinking about a doctor inserting a huge needle into Mary's uterine cavity to take cells from the fluid around the baby terrifies me. The fetus could be damaged; there could be an unexpected loss of amniotic fluid; or, even worse, a uterine infection could develop, ending the pregnancy.

Should I consult with Mary, or is it better to exclude her from such decisions? It's my baby, but it's her body. I don't want to set a precedent, and my dilemma lies in whom to consult: there is no reference book for these topics, and the agency is not the best option. If I include the staff there, I could lose control. The contract gives me the authority to make any decision to protect the life of the baby or, in the event of a genetic problem, even terminate the pregnancy. But this isn't a legal issue; it's a matter of courtesy. What parameters should I establish, now that we've entered the second trimester, the decisive one?

Gonzalo and I are leaning toward selective type tests. Because of the medical complexity, we feel that the obstetrician-gynecologist must take the lead. We will follow his instructions. What other option do we have? The tests we decide to do include a fetal neck test, which analyzes the nuchal fold thickness, and a so-called triple screen, a blood test that determines the levels of alpha-fetoprotein, hCG, and estriol. If the alpha-fetoprotein is low in relation to Mary's age, this indicates a risk that the baby may have Down syndrome. With regard to hCG, the hormone secreted by the placenta, it should ideally remain low in the blood; if not, that could signal a possible genetic alteration. Estriol, which is produced both by the placenta and by the fetus, should not be low, because too little would lead to future problems for the baby.

None of these tests can indicate, with absolute certainty, that the baby will be born lacking one chromosome or with one extra, but they will alert the doctor to any possible anomaly, which will in turn signal the need for more conclusive tests.

We'll receive some of the results in the next few days; the rest will reach the doctor after at least two weeks. The endless waiting is gut-wrenching. Nothing is immediate. Nothing is concrete. Nothing is tangible. Nothing is safe.

Gonzalo and I decide to start calling the baby by its name. If it's a boy, he will be Lucas, which is my middle name. I was born on Saint Lucas Day. We look for the name's meaning: "the one who shines." I've always wanted to have a son with that name. We also like Oliver: "the one who brings peace." I would like to combine Lucas with Andrea, my mom's first name. Or David, Alexander, Marco.

If it's a girl, Gonzalo will decide her name. I like Elisa, Anna, Elise, Sofía, Isabel, Inés, Lucía, Eugenia, Nadia. But Gonzalo has always had a soft spot for Emma. The name's origin is Hebrew, a diminutive of Emmanuela. In its Germanic form, it personifies a strong, gentle, and fraternal woman. For the Greeks, Emma means "she who has grace." Among the Catholic saints, her celebration is on February 1. Saint Emma was extremely generous; she dedicated herself to helping the poor. Even better, the name sounds the same in English and Spanish. And it's easy to spell. But there are too many Emmas. If we go with this name, she should have a middle name too. How about Isabella? Too pretentious. Isabel. I prefer Isabel, "the one who loves God."

Emma? My mom surveys the family and claims that "nobody likes it." My sister thinks that Emma is an older lady's name, my mother reports; even cousin Iliana thinks it sounds strange. They don't understand. This is not a survey, this is a fact: if it's a boy, he will be Lucas Gonzalo. If it's a girl, Emma Isabel. The family will get used to it. Then I remember *Angel of the Waters* in Central Park and its creator, Emma Stebbins. And the protagonist of Flaubert's masterpiece, *Madame Bovary*. Those are signs that we won't ignore.

Emma Isabel. Done.

For Mother's Day, Gonzalo and I fly my mom to Los Angeles. The surprise is that from there we'll drive to La Mesa, just east of San Diego, with Esther María and Néstor, her husband. We'll attend the sixteen-week ultrasound appointment, and if the baby is in the right position, we'll find out its gender for sure.

When my mom learns that she's finally going to meet Mary, she's excited. She makes a quick shopping trip and fills a bag with gifts for her and her daughter. She doesn't know how else to thank her.

THE APPOINTMENT IS at noon, and we arrive early at the office, located in a side building of the Women's Health Center at Sharp Grossmont Hospital, where my baby will be born.

Five of us, plus Mary of course, have come to witness the ultrasound that will allow us to choose a name.

"The whole family! I'm going to have to find the biggest room so that you all fit," the receptionist said cheerfully. She's the mother of one of the nurses who works with Dr. Wood.

I think Mary is a little taken aback when everyone steps over to hug her. She wasn't expecting it. Gonzalo explains the traditional way to determine a baby's gender. You take a very long hair, tie it to a ring that's dropped like a pendulum toward the pregnant woman's belly, and watch what it does. If the ring moves in a circular way, it's a girl; if it moves in a straight line, it's a boy. Mary looks at him with an expression that seems to say, "What is he talking about?"

Everyone comments that she's already showing. I actually believe she just enjoys wearing baggy tops. Her belly is still small, to my eyes.

On the monitor, we can see the baby's skull and spine, and at times it seems as if it's sucking its thumb. It's in constant motion. The technician measures it, makes calculations. Is everything okay?

"So far, it's a sixteen-week-old baby, very well formed. Do you want to know the sex?"

A chorus of yeses.

"Well, it seems that it's a girl."

Esther María begins to cry. Néstor hugs her. My mom is moved. I'm in shock. I sense Gonzalo behind me, inching closer. He grabs my hand and gives it a firm squeeze. I turn and hug him. His heartbeat synchronizes with mine. He smiles. It's becoming ever more real that we're going to be dads. In fact, we already are. We're with our daughter in the same room, never before as close as today.

The technician moves the transducer over Mary's abdomen

and shows us her kidneys, her heart. She stops the image and writes on the screen: "She is definitely a girl."

She prints the image, hands it to us. We'll be leaving with a close-up of my Emma. I say my daughter's name out loud.

"Oh, is she an Emma? What a beautiful name," says the technician. It's clear that our daughter is not the first Emma that she's received in her office.

A girl. I leave a message at the clinic for Dr. Wood. I hug Mary.

Emma Isabel. The name is already familiar to me. My daughter exists. With each step forward she's more concrete. She's no longer an illusion. Now, off to tour La Jolla and celebrate.

BABY CORREA

I LIVE IN A PERMANENT state of unease these days. Every time I email or message Mary and it takes her twenty-four hours or more to reply, I can't help but worry.

We're going to dinner with some friends and I can't stop checking my messages. I can't fully participate in any conversation. All my topics revolve around the baby we're expecting.

We're halfway there. Mary is twenty weeks pregnant. The baby is already ten inches tall, coated in fatty substance, the vernix caseosa, which protects her skin in the amniotic fluid and which, at the time of delivery, works as a lubricant.

She's already capable of hearing too. For now, she must settle for Mary's heartbeat. The next time we meet, I'll speak loudly so that she starts to get used to my voice. I wonder what Mary tells Emma? Do they talk? And does Mary's little daughter communicate with her?

The last I heard from Mary is that she felt the baby moving. My daughter has thrown her first kick, apparently. That's it, Mary didn't go into details: I don't know how long the movement lasted, or if it has happened again. My baby's already doing her thing, imposing herself and sending signs when she's hungry, she's uncomfortable, or she doesn't like the music that Mary's listening to. She's already defending herself.

Sitting on a bench at the San Diego train terminal, I busy myself with the fundamental occupation of the last few months: waiting. I've learned that time is a space to which we belong and which we rarely leave. We are time. Having accepted that, I've also learned to avoid despair. In an instant, life can change, but an instant can also feel like an eternity. Mary agreed to pick me up at the station so that we can head over to her monthly checkup together, followed by an ultrasound appointment. She's fifteen minutes late. All I can do is leave her a message saying I'm already in San Diego.

Finally Mary drives up in her new black truck, beaming. She definitely looks pregnant now. Her hair is down and she's wearing makeup. The earrings I gave her for Mother's Day dress her in an air of femininity. She says she loves them, everybody compliments her on them.

The obstetrician has plenty of good news. There's no need to do an amniocentesis. The triple screen test results were normal. There are no neural tube defects, no danger of the baby having Down syndrome, and no extra material from chromosome 18, a fairly common anomaly that prevents a baby from developing normally.

After the monthly checkup, we continue to a clinic in La Jolla to get a 4D ultrasound. This is a new procedure for us: it will allow me to better see what my daughter looks like, how she moves. We may be able to get a more detailed profile: her little nose, her mouth, her eyes, the shape of her head. It's still a bit early, they tell me, to get a complete image.

However, there she is, with her hand on her cheek, as if she were resting; then she sucks her thumb and falls asleep. She doesn't want to move.

THE TIME HAS come to go to court and request a paternity order before a judge. Even more so now that I've seen my girl in motion. I've filled out all the required documentation and sent it to my attorney in advance. From before Emma is born, she must be legally acknowledged as mine. Mary relinquishes her rights and the document is subsequently sealed, so that no public record shows the procedure through which we created Emma, nor the names of the egg donor and the gestational mother. I must present that legal order at the hospital for them to process the birth certificate with only my name.

I'm eager to see the first document where my baby is referred to as Emma, but we'll have to wait on that, my lawyer says. He tells me that, for legal procedures, she will continue to be Baby Correa.

Every time Mary tells me that she felt a kick or that the baby wouldn't let her sleep, she refers to her as Baby Correa. It's our code. My daughter will be Emma Isabel the day we meet. That moment is drawing closer. For now, I'm fine with her being my Baby Correa.

But I ask her to behave, not to bother Mary so much. Today, in addition to singing her to sleep, I will read her a story.

One of those that begin with *Once upon a time . . .*

I HARDLY EVER see single dads with their children at shopping malls. A few might be spotted over a weekend, but those few almost always have a boy instead of a girl. If they go with a six-, seven-, or eight-year-old girl, what do they do if they have to take her to the bathroom?

I'll figure out a way. It's a minor concern. Similar concerns will follow. The first period, clothes, hairstyles, dolls, friends, boyfriends. I'm going to have a baby who will quickly turn into a girl and, next thing we know, a teenager. In the blink of an eye, she'll be a woman. Oh my God. Will she feel the absence of a mother? Will we be able to be both father and mother? At bedtime, I'm going to sing to her. It is and will be my nightly routine. I'll read her favorite stories. We'll talk about school, about what she learned, about her friends, about her fears. We will be very close.

I've always believed that one misses most what one loses. Emma won't have lost a mother: she will have gained two fathers. I know there are many types of family. I myself have not had a conventional one. With love, everything can be resolved, and we will devote all of our time to her.

She has yet to be born, and—at a distance—that baby is already the center of our lives.

KICKING

AUGUST 2005

THE DAY BEFORE I fly to San Diego for another ultrasound, I'm scheduled to interview Ricky Martin. I feel like I have two full-time jobs: director of the Emma project and magazine editor.

We're scheduled to meet at a photo studio in Miami Beach. The photographer, makeup artist, and stylist are ready when I arrive. We have only two hours for the photos and interview. This is a special edition, so everything must go perfectly.

It's not the first time that I've come face to face with Ricky, or the first time that he's answered my questions. At times I'm incisive, but he knows there is always a measure of respect. I've tried to gain his trust in the past by publishing his statements verbatim, to avoid crossing barriers that could endanger his privacy. Joselo, his right-hand man and one of his most faithful friends, welcomes me with his usual camaraderie and tells me that Ricky is ready.

When Ricky joins us, I sense that he's alarmed: fame makes people vulnerable. A celebrity of his caliber has to learn to distrust, to protect himself even from his own shadow. Anyone can betray him. Even his closest ally can unscrupulously sell him out.

To break the ice, or perhaps because these days I have a one-track mind, I tell him about my project. My daughter is due in November, I say; her name will be Emma Isabel. Mary is the gestational mother. Karen was the egg donor . . .

Ricky is stunned. He doesn't bother me with questions. In fact, I've given him all the answers. Joselo is also amazed and doesn't stop congratulating me. We spend more than half the time scheduled for the interview discussing surrogacy and the laws in California. After that lead-in Ricky seems much more relaxed. He answers my questions honestly; the photo shoot flows smoothly. Wrapping up, I think I flummoxed Ricky that day. And I could have kept going if necessary: I had the sixteen-week ultrasound image with me, but didn't venture to show it to him.

Gonzalo and I certainly admire that image often enough, and we speculate about what our baby is up to. Early in the pregnancy, we used to dream of the baby moving. I'd call Mary every week for her to tell me if she felt kicks, but it's no longer newsworthy; now the baby doesn't stop moving.

When I join Mary in San Diego for the next ultrasound, she says our daughter moves tirelessly. The baby lets her know if she's hungry, thirsty, sleepy, or wants to get some fresh air. With one kick, she controls the universe around her. Mary shows me how her belly's distorted and how it goes from being round to pointed or vice versa in seconds in response to activity within. At times the baby's movements are so strong that they leave Mary gasping for air.

The ultrasound is reassuring. Emma now has eyebrows and eyelashes, and her heartbeat is getting stronger. She's running out of space in Mary's womb. She must be eager to get out, but I ask her to remain calm, tell her that we'll be meeting soon.

Mary can feel our daughter's body, feel her every movement. I envy her so much. Sometimes she feels as if Emma's ready to get out *now*. In my prayers, I ask for calm; all in due time. May Emma continue to grow and develop: we're already in the final stretch.

Our friend Laura calls the next day at dawn. She's pregnant. She's going to be a single mom.

CONTRACTIONS

SEPTEMBER 2005

Every hour that passes confirms that I'm already a father, even though I still don't have Emma in my arms and we're separated by a placenta, a foreign womb, and thousands of miles. Distance is an abstraction. I can already feel her, speak to her, see her. Nothing and no one can separate me from her.

Another month, another ultrasound. Emma is thirty-two weeks old today, she weighs about five pounds, and her feet are two and half inches long. She's going to be very tall, apparently. The ultrasound technician confirms it; she smiles and begins to analyze the heartbeat. From now on, the baby will gain half a pound a week, we're told, and already occupies all the uterus. Even her nails are formed.

Mary has begun to feel contractions, the so-called Braxton Hicks variety, albeit sporadically. The doctor tells us that she's one centimeter dilated. Almost there? Are we having a premature baby? As desperate as I am to meet you, I'm convinced that I must be patient, especially in this final stretch. Your lungs aren't yet fully developed, and we must avoid any complications. There's still a ways to go from the one centimeter of dilation to the ten that you need to be born. That single centimeter needs to hold steady in the following week's checkup. Nothing less or more, the doctor warns us.

Mary has reached the stage where she feels tired. Does she regret this? I don't think so. Her perennial smile, always talking about her daughter, shows that she's satisfied. She's probably eager to shed the weight that has affected her back, eager to be rid of the bad nights, the incessant kicking. "Almost there" is the only comfort I can give her. A month and a half more, and goodbye.

Each week now the doctor will check Mary's cervix, which should soften, and will let us know when Emma will be ready to arrive. Optimally, that won't be until at least the thirty-sixth week. The prudent thing to do, the doctor says, is to set the date for labor to be induced, so that we can make arrangements. After you're born, we'll have to stay in California for at least ten days. It's the time required by the airlines before a newborn is allowed to fly.

We need a hotel. But we first need to decide whether we'll drive with you to Los Angeles or stay in San Diego or La Mesa, near the hospital. I make several reservations at hotels in the area between November 1 and November 14.

I feel as if you're about to arrive. Will I be ready? I've never changed a diaper. We'll manage.

We stop in at the Sharp Grossmont Hospital Women's Health Center, where you'll be born. The rooms are private and, if the delivery has no complications, you'll be born in the same bed where Mary will have proceeded through labor. It's a very relaxed atmosphere. The family will have access to the childbirth. Then you, along with your two dads, will be moved to a suite where we will stay for two days.

I sign all the necessary documents and leave a copy of the

paternity order, as the original must be in my possession on the day of birth. A social worker takes care of us and gives us a tour of the various rooms. We're officially registered now. Mary is the gestational mother, it's clear; and I am the father, the only one with rights to Baby Correa.

As we pass by one of the birthing rooms, the door closes and a red light comes on, like the one at television studios when a live program is taking place. A child is about to be born. On the way back, the door is open again and the baby's cry is heard. Another door closes and another red light comes on. My heart beats faster. A man sitting on a sofa is crying and avoids making eye contact with us. The social worker smiles to ease the tension. I want to know who he is, what's wrong with him, how his child is doing.

We estimate that at least five children were born during our visit. Gonzalo has filmed everything, of course. He follows us with the camera around every corner. At first, Mary looks a bit uncomfortable with the attention, but then she relaxes. She even smiles and poses for him.

At the exit there's a small shop where people can order flowers for the due date. There are also postcards, stuffed animals. The surrogacy agency recommends giving jewelry to the gestational mother. It can be a necklace, some earrings. I think the best thing to do is buy Mary some pearl earrings from Tiffany's. They're elegant and at the same time simple.

Along with an arrangement of red roses, she'll receive the little blue Tiffany's box with the white ribbon and a dedication from the three of us—because by then, you will already be born, Emma: "To the most wonderful woman in the world. Indebted to you for life."

THE LAST TRIP

I'M TURNING FORTY-SIX YEARS old today. My daughter will be born in about three weeks. My family throws us a farewell party that is more like a welcome one. They've all brought presents for Emma. Tomorrow Gonzalo and I fly to San Diego.

At La Ideal, a baby store in Miami, we recently bought the going-home outfit that Emma will wear when leaving the hospital. The saleswoman warned us that it had to be yellow. She had two daughters, she told us, one of whom she'd dressed in white, and "to this day she has very bad luck." She dressed the youngest in yellow, and she's a winner. Yellow is the color of the Virgen de la Caridad del Cobre, the patron saint of Cuba, which explains this Cuban tradition. We buy a pair of socks, pants, a dress, a hat, a blanket. All yellow.

I don't want my girl to enter the world on the wrong foot. Luck will be with her. We went through too much work searching for her, and I'm not about to make a random mistake.

It has been a unique year. Looking back, I can't believe what we've been through. Wrong test, forgotten agency, donor without eggs, unwanted pregnancy, lost embryo transfer, and tens of thousands of dollars.

But we are now close. Here, in this house, we will create a home. I think of Emma's room next to ours, her first toys, our first years together.

The house already has a rocking chair, rattles, dolls, dresses, diapers, colored sheets, little gold earrings, silver crucifixes, little pink shoes.

During our farewell party, we all sit in the living room as I present the images I've compiled on the TV. I've titled them "In Search of Emma," and they're a record of our entire process: the meeting with Karen, the day we met Mary, the first ultrasound, the first 4D image, the hospital where Emma will come into the world. The soundtrack is by Nina Simone. Our guests say that Emma and I look alike. That we have the same nose.

The images disappear and the music remains. To be continued: the next chapter will be your arrival.

It's past midnight and the guests haven't left yet. We still have to finish packing. Our girl hasn't been born, but she already has her first suitcase.

Gonzalo and I will stay in Los Angeles until we can bring you home. It will be another long wait. When we return, there will be three of us. My mom reminds me of this. Life can change in a second, and that instant is around the corner.

MARY IS THIRTY-SIX weeks along now. She's still one centimeter dilated, which is normal, and her birth canal is 50 percent formed. On the obstetrician's recommendation, we decide to induce labor on November 14. Mary is due to arrive at the Women's Health Center at 5:30 a.m. She will be given an epidural, and by roughly 4:00 p.m., I will hold Emma in my arms. Mary's belly is huge and much lower. Last night she thought that Baby Correa was going to barge her way out because she wouldn't stop kicking.

The night before, we will all stay at a hotel five minutes from the hospital so that we can arrive early. We'll give Mary time to prepare, and will spend the rest of the day with her until she reaches ten centimeters of dilation.

Mary's mother, Diana from Surrogate Alternatives, and Suham (the clinic's receptionist) will be with her that day too. Suham is also about to give birth. It's the fourth time that she carries the child of intentional parents. In one of the births, she had twins.

For now, though, we're in Los Angeles, where I'll be working from Esther María's house. To edit the magazine articles I'm responsible for, I will have to focus; in addition, I want to coordinate at least two covers, because when my daughter is born, I will disconnect from the office for two months.

Marisela, Gonzalo's other sister, and Fabrizio, her husband, have flown in from Italy. Marisela is an actress, and she's going to perform with her group at the International Latino Theatre Festival of Los Angeles. They'll go with Esther María and Néstor to San Diego on the day of the birth. My sister will come stay with us at the hotel to help. My mom will wait for us in Miami.

We've decided that, two days after the delivery, we'll head to a hotel in Arcadia, near Esther María's house. We had planned to stay close to Mary, so that the separation wouldn't be so abrupt, but then we thought that we'd probably feel uncomfortable, and so would she.

One option is for Mary to pump her breast milk to feed the baby for the first few days, and we'll combine it with formula. We need to figure all that out by November 14. For now, we can only wait.

These days, Mary is more sensitive. We keep in touch all the time. She tells us how much the baby moves at night, if she lets her sleep, the heartburn she causes. Anything Mary eats fills her up too much, and every night her daughter sings Baby Correa to sleep. I do too. I haven't stopped doing it.

THE DAY BEFORE

NOVEMBER 13, 2005

THIS IS THE LAST night. Tomorrow we will be three.

I close my eyes and see the ocean before me. I wake up in the hotel's small dark room. When I close my eyes again, I find myself forgotten in the sand on an empty beach.

I was walking barefoot along the shore, attempting to look for my daughter on the horizon, yet unable to detect her. The waves didn't allow it. Every time I thought I'd found her, the rhythmic movement of the huge blue mass erased her from my sight. At one point, I managed to spot her. She was waiting for me; she was floating adrift.

I took off my clothes and swam toward her for over an hour, soon gasping for air. The water was freezing and so dense that I could no longer feel my body. My arms had no more strength, my heart was beating weakly, I was on the verge of losing my pulse. My eyes began to cloud, and in that instant, I managed to reach her. She looked at me and smiled. I couldn't make out her face anymore. Her features had been more precise at a distance; up close, she began to fade.

We both felt that the effort—the water, the waves, the

exertion—had been worth it. She looked at me compassionately: my daughter sympathized with me. We didn't talk. We didn't need to say a word to each other.

The waves gradually calmed and we could float without difficulty. It was around four in the afternoon. It was no longer cold, but we were alone. No one could rescue us.

The challenge now was to get back to shore.

Now, awake, I try to focus on the scene and am unable to see how it ends. I'm in the middle of the ocean with my newborn daughter. There is no turning back: we're together, even if our fate is to remain adrift.

Rolling over in bed, I realize with joy that the years of searching and unrest have come to an end. Emma is soon, very soon, going to be my reality, not my dream. I've learned to heal without scars; I can forget the nightmares. What matters is that, in a matter of hours, I will have her in my arms.

Though hours remain of this night, I think about the day to come. I will have to decide what clothes to wear, how I want to look when Emma first sees me. I must rehearse my upcoming encounter with my daughter, to avoid mistakes. What am I going to say when I see her for the first time? I want her to hear my voice as soon as she's born. I want to make the most of her wide-open eyes as we look at and recognize each other. Suddenly I know what to say.

At that precise moment, when she's nice and close to me, I'll whisper in her ear that I'm her father, that I've done everything in my power to bring her into the world ever since I dreamed of her on the last night of the previous century, and that I'll never leave her side. I'll show her to Mary, and we'll say our goodbyes. Someday, when she's older, I'll tell her how we conceived her with the help of two wonderful women. But that is still a long while away.

Then I will ask her to close her eyes and rest from the effort she made to detach herself from Mary's womb. I will sing to her softly, my lips very close to her face. When she wakes up, she'll see me, because I will be there, as always.

Duérmete mi niña, duérmete mi amor, duérmete pedazo, de mi corazón.

MEETING EMMA

NOVEMBER 14, 2005

WE ARE MEETING TODAY. According to the doctor, at about four in the afternoon. Just like that, as if it were nothing, as if everything had been decided yesterday. The truth is that our encounter has been years in the making, at times on the brink of collapse, occasionally with little hope, but always with the certainty that in the end I would hold Emma in my arms. And today is the day. I still can't get used to the idea. Walking into the hospital empty-handed and leaving with her.

During my wakeful time last night I practiced what I'm going to say to her; now I try to imagine how she'll react to my voice. I'm wearing a red shirt, for our good luck. Can she already distinguish colors? Or is it still too soon?

It's seven in the morning and Mary is already in bed at the hospital: her water has broken, regular contractions have started, and the epidural is ready to be administered when needed. Her mother is next to her. Gonzalo and I are like two strangers waiting on the sidelines.

How will Mary feel about letting Emma go after having my baby in her womb for nine months? Will she be ready to give her to me, to let her go? Gonzalo has the photo and video cameras ready. He's happy.

Two centimeters. With the water broken, four centimeters. Every hour, one more centimeter of dilation. Emma has heard my voice every time I've been in town, but will that be enough?

The nurse returns, and after another strenuous contraction, the dilation reaches five centimeters. I'm attached to my phone. In Miami, my sister and mom are as aware of the dilation and heartbeat as I am. Six centimeters. My sister says that the jump from six to ten centimeters comes faster. At ten, Emma will be ready for the final push, ready to emerge and let out the scream that will fill her little lungs with air.

They tell me that she's well positioned, headfirst in the birth canal.

Seven centimeters. Never before has counting been so exhausting.

Every time Mary has a contraction, zero hour draws nearer. I'm next to her, and I perceive her effort. The baby's head pops out and back in. With each attempt, the momentum grows. We're together in this battle, Mary and Emma and I. And I know that my daughter wants to come out and meet me.

Eight centimeters. Her heartbeat is getting stronger.

Despite the high expectations, we're all calm. Mary looks tired, and the decisive moment has yet to come. Her mother stands by her side, checks her phone, knits. It's the first time we've seen her. At first she disagreed with Mary's decision to be a surrogate mother. Then she told her it was her decision. But now, when it really matters, she's next to her.

Nine centimeters. We're in the final stretch. I leave the room, walk down the long hall, and listen to the newborns crying.

Ten centimeters. I must go back inside with Mary. One contraction and I can already see the baby's black hair. Another contraction and it looks like she's going to come out. Where's the doctor?

The nurse continues assisting Mary with her labor—suddenly, in a matter of moments, that placid room is turned into a small operating room. The staff warn me that I can't touch anything that's covered with a blue cloth. The doctor arrives; the neonatologist comes over with an incubator. Everything is ready.

"Who's going to cut the umbilical cord?" the doctor asks, looking around him. He seems surprised to see me crying.

I can't answer, but I lift a hand. Gonzalo warns me that I'm going to miss it, but I can't stop crying. I want to show my daughter how happy I am, but tears prevail.

I stand to the doctor's left, ready to cut the only thing that ties my daughter to Mary.

We are in the final stage. Everything in the room comes to a standstill. I check out the serious face of the doctor and his team, geared up in case of any emergency. Those final seconds feel eternal. I'm riveted. I want to grab Mary's hand, but I don't dare. Her mother wipes the sweat from her forehead. Mary scrunches her expression with all her strength, holds her breath, exhales a slight moan, and out comes Emma's little wrinkled face.

Now come the shoulders, then the arms and legs—the whole body at almost the same time.

A soft cry is heard. I wait for her scream, the alarm, lungs filling with air.

I cut the cord and the doctor shows me the miracle.

"She's a beautiful baby," he says.

Next the neonatologist takes Emma in her arms to clean her, weigh her, swaddle her.

"Seven pounds and seven ounces," she declares.

"Lucky number," adds the obstetrician with a wide smile.

Now the newcomer begins to cry with all her might. The

neonatologist assures us that that's the sound she's been waiting for. My daughter adopts an angry expression that makes the
nurse laugh. "Emma, you're a drama queen!" she says.

The nurse then puts a bracelet with my daughter's name on
my left wrist. Gonzalo gets one too.

Mary looks at us, pleased. Her mother begins to cry. I pat
Mary's head to convey our thanks.

And for the first time, I take my baby, wrapped in the usual
blanket for newborns, in my arms.

"Welcome, Emma. I'm your dad," I whisper in her ear, my
voice cracking. "I love you with all my heart, and have since the
day I dreamed of you."

Her huge wide eyes watch me as if she understands what I'm
murmuring. As if she recognizes the voice that's been singing to
her for months from the other side of the country.

Gonzalo continues to film, we hug each other, and I say to
Emma, "Gonzalo is also your dad."

She stares at me as I carry her to a corner of the room so that
I can contemplate her calmly, outline her face, let her little hands
hold my finger as if she doesn't want to let me go.

Mary's husband and her young daughter arrive; when Gonzalo and I are told that our room is ready, we say an emotional
goodbye to Mary and her family. Once we're alone, we check her
over, we admire her, we change her first diaper while she pouts
and looks up at us in amazement. I give her the first feeding of
formula, which she drinks with enthusiasm.

When the social worker arrives, we fill out all the information for our daughter's birth certificate: "She was born on November 14, 2005, in La Mesa, California," I say formally. The social
worker writes the baby's name: Emma Isabel Correa. She writes
my name: Armando Lucas Correa. And in the section where
the name of the baby's mother should appear, only one word:
"Unknown."

ANNA AND LUCAS

FOUR YEARS LATER

I CLOSE MY EYES AND once again see the ocean before me. I can't believe that in a few hours, there will be five of us. When I wake up from my dozing, I'm thirty thousand feet in the air, away from Emma. Anna and Lucas are about to be born, may have already been born. And I'm flying between New York (once again our home) and San Diego, equidistant from my daughter and my new babies, surrounded by more than two hundred strangers to whom I cannot yell that my twins are coming into the world.

LET'S BACK UP half a day.

I already know that everything can change in a second. No doubt about it. Today my life will take a 180-degree turn. All plans have come undone: Anna and Lucas should have been born on December 30, two weeks before the standard forty because they're twins. Mary has been feeling fine, she's been having a smooth pregnancy, but today—Sunday, December 13—everything changes.

After waking up and going about my morning routine, I check my phone and see a missed call from Mary. I try to get through to her, but her voicemail picks up. I look for Gonzalo's phone and see that he also has a missed call. Something is up. It's too early for her, in Pacific time. It must be six, seven in the morning over there . . .

I definitely have to find her. I wake Gonzalo to tell him that something is happening, that I keep trying to locate Mary unsuccessfully. When we most need it, the phone doesn't work. She's out of range, perhaps. What do I do?

Finally, Mary answers. "I woke up wet. Not much, but I think my water broke. I called the doctor and he told me to go to the hospital. Don't worry: I feel fine, the children are moving. I have no pain, and at the moment, no contractions . . ."

I sit down and take a deep breath. I must get a ticket to San Diego as soon as possible. The whole family was planning to fly out on December 20; we booked the hotel near the hospital to be close for the birth and rented a house in Pasadena for when the babies were discharged. My mother, sister, Aunt Ibis, Gonzalo's sisters, and their husbands were coming too. The whole family would celebrate the end of 2009 with the arrival of Anna and Lucas.

The plan has suddenly changed. I rush to the office: I must finish my editorial column for the magazine. We're about to close that edition. In other words, I have to approve the pages and the cover before I go. I work quickly, then write a note to my boss and my team: "My children are about to be born."

Mary gets in touch once she's at the hospital. Lucas's water broke, she says, but Anna's is still intact. Everything is under control, but she doesn't think the doctors will wait until tomorrow to perform a C-section.

I find a direct flight to San Diego from Newark, leaving at six in the afternoon. I barely have time to pack and head for New Jersey.

Esther María, Gonzalo's sister, and Néstor, her husband, are driving from Los Angeles to the San Diego area and will be with Mary in case of an emergency C-section.

"Wait for me, please!" I implore Mary, and relaxed as always, she calms me with her sweet voice.

It's SIX IN the afternoon and my flight is about to leave. Just before takeoff, as I'm about to put my phone into airplane mode, I get a call from my friend Norma Niurka.

Norma has been battling cancer for two years, and we talk almost every day. Each time she's admitted to the hospital, she calls me, as if to say goodbye. She talks to me softly, and is happy to know that the twins are on their way. She whispers her usual, "Ay, Mandy . . ." and sighs. I must hang up; within minutes the plane begins to gain altitude.

Five and a half hours later, I land in San Diego. It's nighttime, and the first thing I do is check my phone, hoping for news. Yes, the babies have already been born: Lucas weighed 6.1 pounds and Anna, 5.9 pounds. Esther María hasn't been able to see them, because only the father is allowed to enter the NICU (neonatal intensive care unit). Even Mary hasn't been allowed in.

I head toward the airport's main entrance and catch sight of Esther María and Néstor; they're picking me up to take me to the hospital—the same one where Emma was born. Once again, we travel to nearby La Mesa, this time with a rush of anxiety beyond my control. I think of my children, alone in a room, without any relative by their side.

When we reach the door, Esther María informs the assistant, "He's the father of the twins!"

After confirming my identity, the woman smiles and congratulates me as she places two bracelets on my wrists: Baby Correa 1 (boy) and Baby Correa 2 (girl).

I rush in and there they are: Anna, asleep and breathing softly under a warming lamp. Lucas, hooked up to wires and surrounded by monitors that control the beating of his little heart. He struggles to fill his premature lungs with oxygen, and his chest sinks as if he's trying to suck in every last drop of air from the room. An oxygen-supplying helmet has been placed on his head to help him breathe. I can't see him, I don't recognize him: Is that my son?

"You'll be able to take the girl in a few hours, after her first feeding. The boy must remain under observation," says the nurse without looking at me, presumably to avoid any reaction. I feel like a spectator at a movie that doesn't include me, at least for now. Everything has happened too fast.

Esther María and Néstor must return to Los Angeles, so I'm on my own. Mary is in another building. Hospital staff tell me that she's fine, although she lost some blood and they had to give her two transfusions. I talk to her on the phone: she's in pain; now she needs to rest.

After midnight a nurse hands me Anna, who is tiny. She nestles in my arm as I give her the first feeding. She manages to drink almost an ounce.

"She's yours. You can take her to your room," says the nurse, who is now looking at me, because she wants to see my expression of happiness. I put Anna to bed in the portable crib that they'll use to move her, and I stay behind for a few seconds to watch Lucas. It's hard to leave him.

The transfer with Anna goes smoothly. I look around at our new quarters, another room at the hospital where Emma came into the world. I relive that day, the happiness that I felt when I saw her and heard her cry for the first time. I couldn't be here for the arrival of Anna and Lucas, but I now have one of my little babies, and I can't wait for everyone to meet her.

I start talking to her, telling her about Emma, Gonzalo. We're alone in the dimly lit room.

At dawn, Marta, a nurse who remembers me from Emma's birth, tells me that I can leave Anna with her to go see Lucas. I jump at the chance and return to the NICU.

"He had a really bad night. We're going to have to intubate him to help him breathe. If we don't, he might stop breathing from exhaustion," explains the doctor as she manipulates the paraphernalia that surrounds my son.

It's now Monday. Anna will be discharged tomorrow. Esther María and Néstor will come help me move to a nearby hotel. Lucas will have to stay in the NICU. On Wednesday, my sister and Ibis will be here to help me. It's hard for me to fathom leaving Lucas alone, among strangers. Until now we've been in the same building; soon we're going to be separated. I still haven't been able to say to him, "I'm your dad, Lucas, and I love you with all my heart." The most I've been able to do is take his little hand. Though my urge to hug him is strong, I know I can't; I don't want to put him at risk with my touch. I want him to get well, to gain strength, to mature so that he can be with his sister and me.

Gonzalo and Emma are trying to change their tickets so they can fly in this weekend. I'll be glad to have their support. I feel completely helpless on my own.

On Tuesday morning, the day of Anna's planned discharge, the doctor calls me on the phone. "Lucas isn't well," she says, and goes quiet. One of those pauses doctors seem to take when they're about to deliver bad news. "We're going to have to put a tube directly into one lung to drain it. It's full of liquid."

I call my sister but can't speak; my crying won't let me. What do I do? I'm desperate, I have to be with Anna—I can't leave her alone—and yet Lucas is on *his* own, in the hands of a doctor who is trying to save his life and whom I have to trust blindly.

Norma calls me. I tell her that I'm alone, that Lucas is very weak, that I haven't properly met him yet.

"I wish I could be there with you to help," my friend replies. "Send me photos as soon as the five of you take one together."

Her voice seems faint, as if she's summoning all of her strength to articulate each word. I know that Norma is also having trouble breathing, that her lungs are working at 30 percent of their capacity, that they fill with fluid and have to be drained constantly. I say goodbye but she's still there, on the other end of the line, as if wanting to join Anna and me and encourage me along.

"Lucas is strong, believe me," she says.

Of course I believe her.

The wood-paneled hospital room that's our home for another couple of hours is huge for the two of us. Anna seems even smaller in this space. Lucas's crib is empty, waiting for him. In the NICU, the doctor says, "We can't have any babies intubated for more than two days," offering no explanation. "If Lucas isn't breathing on his own by tomorrow, we'll have to transfer him to another hospital."

After her discharge, Anna and I move to a hotel, one that's five minutes from Lucas. We spend the first night alone. How long has it been since I've slept through the night? Anna must be fed every two hours, and the milk-drinking process can take an hour.

My sister and Ibis arrive the next day, allowing me to spend more time with Lucas. Ibis accompanies me to the hospital to see how he's doing. He will soon breathe on his own, I believe. *Come on, Lucas, you can do it. Be strong. I'm sorry for making you suffer. I never imagined you'd come early. I thought you'd stay inside Mary until you were ready to breathe outside. Together, we will win this battle.*

"An ambulance is going to transfer Lucas to Mary Birch

Hospital in San Diego," a staff member informs me, and I receive the news like a slap in the face. The doctor is manipulating Lucas: I see tubes that are put in and out, needles that switch places, IVs that are emptied and exchanged for others. "The hospital is thirty minutes from here," the doctor adds. "He may need a blood transfusion en route."

I'm sitting in front of Lucas, grasping his little hand, and the nurse gives me a photo that they took in the NICU: his first image. They allow me to say goodbye. I get really close to him for the first time—I can feel his heartbeat—and I tell him that we're never going to be apart, that the whole family is thinking about him. Feeling disoriented, I'm brought back to reality when they make me sign a document stating that Lucas may die in the transfer to the other hospital, that they can't be held responsible.

In tears, I follow Lucas and the paramedics. People waiting in the hospital lobby look at me with concern.

A nurse hugs me and assures me that Lucas will be fine, but I keep crying inconsolably. I *know* that he will be cured, I have no doubt about that, but seeing him suffer fills me with despair.

We arrive at the new hospital, where the NICU is one huge room with more than sixty children. The infant warmers are lined up, one next to the other. Lucas has a single nurse dedicated to him twenty-four hours a day.

"His lungs are clear," the nurse tells me. "We'll most likely remove his tube tomorrow." The good news has begun.

Oh God, finally my son is progressing. I've seen his face for the first time. I begin to recognize him.

The next day, my mother arrives and we go visit Lucas together. His nurse allows me to hold him, and I feel like he was born today. He still has an umbilical venous line in his navel through which they feed him, but I'm able to hold him in my arms for three hours straight. I can't believe it.

I hesitantly ask the nurse, who begins to bathe him with a damp cloth, when she thinks he will be discharged.

"Take it easy," she advises. "It's a slow process. We want him to be completely fine when he leaves. He may be able to move to an intermediate care room in a few days, where he'll be in a crib."

THE TIME I spent away from Emma felt like an eternity. I'm in the hotel parking lot waiting for her to arrive now. I see her get out of the car with Gonzalo and she runs toward me. We all hug and catch up on what's been happening.

Emma is still not allowed to visit Lucas, but she's entranced by Anna as soon as they meet. She glances at the infant as if wondering, *So this is my little sister?* Soon the little one will laugh just by looking at Emma. Soon she will reach out to her. Soon she will adore and pester her older sister. They will make each other laugh and accompany each other everywhere.

Lucas goes to intermediate care after the few days the nurse predicted. I give him his first feeding and he devours it. He's swallowing and breathing perfectly. We're already in a room with apparently healthy babies. Soon we will get go home—or rather, to the hotel that will be our home for several more weeks.

Two days before Christmas, Lucas is discharged. Gonzalo and Emma pick us up. Lucas is beyond endearing.

We have dinner as a family the next day. Esther María and Néstor have brought the traditional Christmas Eve meal from Los Angeles, and they spend the night at the hotel. The next morning, the first thing I do is dress the babies in Christmas clothes: Anna in red and Lucas in green. We take the first photo of the five of us together and I send it to my friend Norma, who must still be in the hospital: "Merry Christmas. See you soon. Here's the photo I promised you."

That image and message travel not just to Norma but to the

world, *our* world. The twins, Anna and Lucas, have been born and are doing well, we announce. The nightmare has passed. We are all together as a family.

At around three in the afternoon, I receive a call from Luisito, Norma's son.

"She left us. Norma has left us," he murmurs.

I don't understand what he's telling me. I'm holding Lucas in my arms, feeding him. I'm a bit distracted. What is he trying to say?

"Norma died."

I have no more questions. I recall our last conversation, her farewell. She knew it would be the last time we would speak and I didn't give her enough time; I didn't call her again, either. I was immersed in my own problems, with Lucas fighting for his life.

"Norma left us," I repeat, adopting Luisito's cipher. To leave. To depart. Sometimes one leaves without saying goodbye. That's how Norma departed. I break the news to everyone. They immediately understand.

WE MOVE TO a hotel in San Diego, as originally planned. Gonzalo's sisters and their families join us. We will ring in the New Year there. Then we will move to the house we rented in Pasadena until we can fly with our newborns.

ON JANUARY 10, almost a month after Anna and Lucas were born, we get on a plane home. There are six of us, including my mother. Gonzalo is sitting with Anna, my mother with Emma, and I'm with Lucas.

The problems are behind us. Who remembers the NICU days? Sometimes I think I've run out of tears.

Mary comes to say goodbye with her daughters. She has

already fully recovered; she's strong. She's glad to finally meet Lucas; after his birth he was rushed away, so she was able to say goodbye only to Anna. Now she kisses him, the last one.

What does Mary feel? How can she cope with separating from these babies after having carried them for nine months in her womb? We had the chance to see her in Miami last fall, six months pregnant with the twins. We talked then, and I was able to better understand her.

She confirms her acceptance now. "Not everyone can be a gestational mother," she explains. "I know that these children are not mine, they're yours. I'm happy to have helped you create your family. Emma and Anna and Lucas will always be part of my life, even if I don't see them. I know they're there, in good hands."

THE PLANE LANDS. It's nighttime; it's cold, the temperature below zero. I look out the window and feel as if I'm facing a new life. I kiss Lucas, I kiss Anna. Emma comes over and hugs me, and I also kiss her. She hugs me and looks intently at me with her usual smile. We both look out the window at the lights of the planes taxiing and taking off. I grab her hand and we get ready to leave.

The process of emptying the plane seems endless, and we're the last out by choice. Once inside the airport, we sit for a moment to regroup. Emma flops down on me and I hold her as if she were still my baby. Lucas and Anna open their eyes and stare at us. Emma smiles at them.

"Now there are five of us, Papá," she says, and kisses me.

This will be a long journey together.

LETTERS

Emma,

I'm going to tell you a story.

A few days before you were born, while we waited happily for your arrival, something magical happened to me. A light entered my crown chakra (the chakra you know), and I awakened. I was introduced to the spiritual world and began to discover something that I did not know: I began to find God.

With that magic light I understood how wonderful human beings are, what we can achieve with Love: unconditional Love, universal Love. Love is the door that leads us to happiness, inner peace. You are a creation of your parents' Love, and that is why you are so exceptional.

With that light I also understood that when a baby is born, it carries within itself a Divine Being, its soul, and chooses the family with whom it wishes to live this physical experience on planet Earth (the planet where you live), and therefore chooses the little body that will serve as a refuge. That is why we are so grateful to you for having selected us as your family.

I realized that babies are born with great wisdom and that they can help their parents with their knowledge. Your parents understand this, and they're giving you the opportunity to fully develop it.

Maintain the connection with your Inner Divine Being and, in this way, you will always be close to the Energy of the creative Source of the worlds, and your life will be as wonderful as you wish.

This is the story I wanted to tell you.

I consider your birth, and that of your cousin Fabián, a gift from God.

Abuelita Niurca

Beautiful Emma,

I've been filled with great joy, tenderness, and peace by the name borne by such a special, sweet, cheerful, and happy little person: you, my granddaughter. You came into my life without even thinking about it. You have been a gift from God. When I found out that you were coming into the world, I was dismayed; I didn't understand how your birth could happen. Then I thought about the happiness that you were going to give your two parents and I understood that your arrival would be a great happiness for them and all of us who love you.

I will always carry within my heart the warm memory of the thirty days that I was by your side. You would take me by the arm and lead me by the hand to the kitchen, early in the morning, to make you breakfast. We both truly enjoyed spending that time together. We sang children's songs that you could barely articulate. Perhaps my future years will not allow me to enjoy your growth, as you have arrived in the twilight of my life to give me warmth, tenderness, and sweetness when I recall the moments experienced with you.

When time passes and I am no longer among all of you, I hope that one day you will think of this grandmother who has always loved and remembered you. If you see a light in a starry night, it is me looking over you and blessing you.

Your abuelita Cuqui, from Cuba

Emma, my little princess,

The day you were born was long awaited. For a while, we watched you grow in photographs and movies. Papá showed us glimpses of your day-today life in Mary's tummy. Then love also grew and became so great that now we cannot see where it ends.

I think about you a lot and sometimes I catch myself playing with you. I take that opportunity to tell you how much I love you and wonder how to attract your attention at least for a little while.

How about we both decide what to do for fun?

Running in the park—we'd like that. But it would be even better if Fabi and your abuela Niurca joined us. How about we tell Papi and Papá to join us too? I'd ask Tía Ibis to bring Simpson—then we'd surely have some fun! We'd carry a ball or balloons, a kite, we'd go to the lake and feed the ducks. They would love for you to give them bread, and of course, we'd eat that bread too.

Do you know what we could do next? Let's see, think about what you'd like. Have a picnic on the grass, make tea, bring cookies.

We could do a lot of fun things like play dominoes, or maybe put together a puzzle.

Meanwhile, why don't we start reading a very long book? So long that it could hide behind the sun. We can go page by page, and it will take some time to finish, so we'll have to plan several picnics together to enjoy that book called "In Search of Emma." See? It has the same name as you, and I think we'll like it.

Invite Papi and Papá, and I'll tell Fabi, your abuela, Tía Ibis—oh, and of course Simpson. Let's read it in the park, between cups of tea and cookies. We will also invite Leonorcita, Valentina, Naomi, Gusti, Emily, Antón, your cousins and friends from Miami.

With all my love, I hug you and jump for joy while I wait to read your book and run together in the park.

Tía Sahily

My dear little cousin Emma,

It's been a long time since I last saw you. Every time you come to visit us, I'm amazed at how you change.

You have gone from being a baby to a girl very quickly. It's been a few years since we met—well, about four.

It has been a long time, and by now you must be immense. Now we love to tell you stories, to see you captivated, but soon enough you will be the one telling us stories.

I love you very much, from the first day I saw you in your dad's arms, when you were just eleven days old and he brought you from San Diego.

Your big cousin, Fabi

Dear Emma,

There are as many children in the world as there are dreams, because each child is a parent's dream, turned into a little person who grows and grows, until they become big.

And you are a great dream woven by your parents.

From the moment you first opened your eyes, tolerance and love merged in a party of colors that lit up the California sky.

I witnessed this because I was there in those autumn days, when your little face came into the world with "scorpionic" subtlety to greet those of us who were eagerly awaiting your arrival.

You were conceived from happiness and to be happy.

So, if you ever feel sad, all you have to do is look up at the sky or paint a rainbow.

There, you will find the right meaning of the word "tolerance."

With lots of love,
Tía Ibis

Pretty Emma,

The night of the day you were born, Tía Mari and Tío Fabrizio, Tío Néstor, and I traveled to a place called La Mesa to meet you. We were somewhat lost on the road, quite nervous because we didn't want to be late to the clinic. But we were late and they told us we couldn't enter. It was ten o'clock at night! Luckily, your dad talked to the nurses and told them that we were coming from far away and that we wouldn't make noise and that we were going to behave. So they put yellow bracelets on us and let us in.

The room was dimly lit and your dad was sitting in an armchair next to your crib, while you slept. You were so small and so pretty that we were speechless observing you. And then we watched you wake up a little, drink milk, go back to sleep. We looked like fools: gazing and gazing at you and taking many photos, as if you were a famous celebrity. Back then, we saw you as the most famous and most important person in the world. Our first niece, the little girl that we had all been waiting for and we could finally meet.

Sometimes when one is very happy, one cries. It's a bit strange, but that's the way it is. And all the aunts and uncles wept, partly from the joy of seeing you and also from the joy of seeing how happy your dads were. We carefully carried you and spoke to you ever so softly so as to not wake you.

Every time I see you, now that you're a big girl, that night comes to mind. Although you already know many things, many letters, many numbers, and you can sing, dance, and make cupcakes, your aunts and uncles still see you as little Emma. That's why we always say: "But this girl is so big! She knows so much!" And we become as happy as if we had just met you.

A big kiss,
Esther María, your tía from California (and another kiss from my dog Henna, who has a lot of fun with you)

My dearest Emma,
You are a beautiful, bright, and friendly three-year-old girl. Your hair shines with a rare beauty.

For you to ask, at your early age, "How many angles does a circle have?" convincingly shows your superior intelligence, especially to a math teacher of many years like me.

The fanciful way with which you select the clothes and accessories you wear daily, the precision that you demonstrate in your ballet steps, and many other examples that I could list are indicative of your great charm.

But not only for the aforementioned do I love, admire, and consider you very important in my life: the happiness that you produce in your father Gonzalo (whom I love not only as my godson but as if he were my own son) makes you a very important human being in my life.

Continue to bring pleasure to your life and that of the many other people who surround and love you: your father Mandy, your many grandmothers and aunts, friends, and more.

I hope that for the rest of my days you continue to be connected to me as your father Gonza has always been.

Your "abuelita" Lydia

Dear Emmita,

On the other side of the ocean from where you live, in a very beautiful country called Italy, which one day you will surely visit, that's where I live. When you lie down on your bed and start to dream, I am waking up to begin a new day. I have a photo of you, and every morning I say good morning to you. Perhaps you may have heard me in your dreams.

I'm overcome with emotion as I write you this letter, the same way I felt the first time I held you in my arms, the day you were born. The joy and happiness of everyone present that night did not fit in the spacious room where you were spending your first hours of life. They were so big even the alarms on the windows began to sound.

You should have seen Papá and Papi; they were beaming, as if they too

had been born with you. You were their longtime great dream. You should
know that to make a dream come true, closing your eyes is not enough. You
must fight with passion, perseverance, strength, and so much love. And this
is what your parents did so that the beautiful girl that you are, ceased to be
a dream.

More than three years have passed since that wonderful day. Now you
are a happy and intelligent girl who is beginning to discover the world with
the naive curiosity of your tender age.

I remember with immense joy the fantastic days we spent together
at your home in New York just a few months ago. I enjoyed you to the
fullest. I close my eyes and feel like I can see you walking with natural
talent around the house in your red heels. I was dying of laughter. Your
contagious smile and your hoarse little voice speaking that Spanish, which
sounded so unique to me: I have them etched in my memory like a great
treasure. And when I'm a little sad, all I need to do is look at the photos
of you and your little cousin Leonorcita to regain peace and happiness.

Thank you, Emma, for making me so happy.

Tía Mary

Cara nipotina Emma,

Small, great star in the sky. The memory of the day you appeared is
connected to a period of great joy for me, due to a coincidence of situations
and happy moments shared with some of the people I love most. That's
why I find it even more beautiful.

I would like the echo of this distant voice to reach you to convey the joy
and beauty that your arrival has brought to the lives of many.

But all words would be in vain, because in the face of beauty and
happiness we humans are usually speechless.

Perhaps images would be more useful: of you looking at the world
around you, curious and funny, and revealing, with your special little being,
tenderness and wonder.

It would be even better explained by the expressions and smiles in the eyes and on the faces of those who, in turn, look at you, accompany you, observe you in awe, and shower you with love. Above all, your parents, who dreamed of you from the beginning and fervently hoped that you would be here, to play and make us play with you in the garden of life.

A poet has said: "It's easy. All you need is love."

As poets are fantastic liars, we believe them, and we know that you will receive infinite love and protection, caresses and dreams, to make you fly over a world where you will need nothing else.

It's easy.

Fabri, your Italian uncle

Dear Emma,

What an afternoon! Three endless hours transpired at the airport. I finally saw my son and after hugging him, practically trembling, another new emotion took hold of me.

We were traveling to his house, and the imminence of the next meeting kept my eyes moist. Finally, in front of me, you and Leonorcita. The two of you looking at me with your doll-like faces in the flesh. Two angels that we had been awaiting for many years were there, observing me.

The smallest, so beautiful, could not yet understand. You, on the other hand, were watching me, between expectant and confused, with your fascinating, mischievous, and eager expression: Who is this old man? They all answered in chorus: "He's your abuelo Gonzalo!" You gave me a shy smile. You probably instinctively felt that this old man was someone else who was there to love you. And this pleased you.

A year and a half have passed since that unforgettable moment, and your photos, which we always look forward to, fill our lives with joy. You're growing up surrounded by a love that you find so easy to return, that you'll surely do so with great intensity when you "grow up." Now, every day, you learn and learn many beautiful things that fill your tender heart.

As the Chinese saying goes: "To be a man you must plant a tree, write a book, and have a child." With all due respect to its author, I allow myself to add: "And have a granddaughter like Emma!"

Abuelo Gonzalo

Emma,

A long time ago I wrote the unfinished story of two men, Liro and Rintumino Doriló, who together were raising a girl named Hebe . . .

I still can't get over the feeling of surprise caused by impossible reunions. This girl is not Hebe, she is Emma. Her parents are really her parents, Mandy and Gonzalo, without the need to be uncles, adoptive parents, or any other type of close relative.

Emma is not a character, she is a real little girl who must have already devoured several pots of milk and reclaimed all of her simplicity in her own way.

As soon as I see you, I will give you a little kiss, Emma. A very nervous little kiss because, as grown-ups, we have become a small piece of time that has come to an eternal standstill in the progression of a specific story, while you, the babies, come from the very secret of time, but you carry it wrapped in an unwavering simplicity.

All right, little one, you will soon get the classic little tickle on your feet . . .

Your tía Sonia María

Dear Emma,

Every day during those nine months, you and Gustavito were the center of our lives. I called your parents every time your cousin did something new in my tummy, or if I felt something strange, because there really came a time when I almost trusted my cousins—your parents— more than my own gynecologist.

Meanwhile, your parents kept me up to date on every change in your short life. After each checkup, we called each other and exchanged the news. Watching the ultrasound videos and then the videos your dad made with so much love, "In Search of Emma" and "In Search of Gustavito or Juliette," became our favorite pastime.

As you can see, four years later, we haven't changed much; you are still the center of our attention. We went from talking about fetal development to diaper changes to choosing the best school for you both.

Sometimes we talk about other things, but we always end up coming back to you both. And that, Emma, will never change. From the day your parents created you, you were, are, and will always be the reason of their lives.

I love you all very much and feel very fortunate and blessed to have been able to share this joy.

Your prima Romy

Emma, my dear goddaughter,

When you are able to read and understand this book and these letters that we have written to you, you will already be a big girl. Your baby teeth will have already fallen out, you will have already had your first day at school, and you will be able to ride at full speed the bicycle that I now promise to buy you.

But if I can give you something of value, of real value in life, it will be to share this with you: I have never met someone who has been so desired, so planned, and as loved as you. And that has made you one of the luckiest girls in the world, one who won the lottery in life, because you live in the hearts of Papá and Papi—as well as in the rest of us, your real and adopted aunts and uncles. You'll know, through words and actions, that you were born and raised surrounded by something that not all children have: love.

I still remember the day Papá entrusted me with his secret plan to have you. To be clear, secret because of the superstition that when you talk about things, they may not happen. In the more than ten years that I had known Papá, I had never seen him like this—so happy, so excited. Well, not until the day you arrived. We were all moved to tears then. And since that happy day, you've only given us more reasons to smile.

I've loved you since before you were born,
Your godmother María

My Emma, my motivation to be a mom,

I began to love you from the moment we toasted with champagne at the home of a friend of your parents. Papá called Papi to tell him you were on your way. We toasted, cried with joy, and from then on, an endless movie began.

Going shopping, thinking of you, talking about what you would be like, who you were going to look like, and watching videos of childbirth that Papá showed us introduced me to a world that I was very afraid of: being a mother.

But that moment came and I will never tire of thanking your dad. I decided to start the beautiful endless journey, the one I always longed for but never stopped fearing. Your dad accelerated my pregnancy when it hadn't even started yet. He could already see me with a baby inside and would tell everyone so.

When it happened, he was the first to receive the news, at six in the morning. We were very happy. I also told him that what was coming for him was the great Emma, because my heart told me that you were going to be a girl.

I remember the day Papi and Papá chose your name. We were in Miami Beach with Richard, a friend of your parents. There, you emerged

as Emma Isabel. We all toasted—as you can see, we toasted very often
because you motivated us, gave us joy.

    You weren't born in Miami, and I already carried your little friend
Valentina inside me. You have no idea how much I suffered that
separation. It was a distant month, yet filled with communication. Your
dad and I talked to each other every day, and I received your first picture.
You were a little doll, so pretty, so beautiful; I was so happy that I felt
Valentina's kicks as signs of love for you.

    You came home to Miami, and when I took you in my arms, it was
wonderful. That's when those nights at seven filled with endless crying
began. One day I picked you up amid one of those cries, went to your
beautiful room, sat down on the armchair, and put you on my belly. I
rocked you and spoke to you softly: in that moment you were also my girl,
I wanted you to feel like Valentina was your little sister, and you fell fast
asleep.

    From then on you started to grow up near me. You no longer sleep in
my arms, but you and Valentina hug each other like great friends do. And
that's because your parents and I adore each other.

    Emma, I don't want you and Valentina to ever part. Both of you were
conceived with a lot of love and you've felt very close to each other since you
were just simple embryos.

We will always be here for you.

Laura and Valentina

Dear Emma,

    This will undoubtedly be one of the most important letters I will ever
write, and it will be a very simple letter, "from an engineer," as your dad
would say.

    I remember when I met you, round and fragile, receiving heaps of love
and returning happiness and joy; above all, I remember the fascination you
produced in your tía Leo, how she lit up and amazed me when she held

you in her arms. I'll tell you something that I've never told anyone: I'm sure
that it was in one of those magical moments, when she carried you and I
watched you two play, that your cousin Leonorcita was born, and not later,
as everyone thinks.

For me you are tenderness, you are my reunion with my childhood
and my desire to have children, you are concern and joy, you are family,
intelligence, and inspiration. You are also a girl, and you will be a very
lucky woman, because life gave you the privilege of having the best parents
in the world, who did everything to have you and will do everything to
make you a happy person.

Last, and most important: you are love. Love made you and love will
always save you.

Your tío Osvaldo

My dear Emma,

I think I was tremendously fortunate to have had the chance to be
present on the days of your conception and at the time of your birth.

One thing became clear to me then: you were a totally modern girl,
a twenty-first-century girl. The scientific and technical conditions and
medical advances that made your existence possible were new in the history
of the world.

But I also understood that, in that moment, social and political
circumstances had made it possible for you to appear among us. Those
conditions, while more difficult to understand, were no less miraculous.
You were a miracle because all life is so, but also because you are a prodigy
of society, the result of the balance between tremendous forces that had
never before been able to agree.

Your parents and your uncles and aunts and grandmothers, we come
from a place where many things were forbidden. One of them was love.
Some people were allowed to lead a full life, with children and family, and
others were not. In order for your parents to love each other and make a

home with a girl like you, they had to cross the sea and come to this side of the Earth.

You should know that this crazy world made peace for you to be born. A new stage in the coexistence of human beings and a more just social contract were your midwives.

For those reasons, I was incredibly proud to meet you that fall morning in San Diego, by the Pacific Ocean, in the West of the movies. I was proud to know that your parents were as brave and true pioneers as those who had conquered those lands many years before. In matters of fatherhood, they founded a new world. They threw themselves into the future, with all its unknowns and all its challenges, only out of love for you, Emma Isabel.

May life bring you long years of happiness!

Now here's a kiss from your tío,
Néstor

My dear niece, Emma,

Someone very dear to me always used to say, "When you have to choose between the heart and reason, always choose the heart, because no one ever regrets choices from the heart." I think you were pure heart, before, during, and after your birth. Your parents chose you and I believe that you also chose them; they wanted you so much and, with them, all of us who love them joined in that unique and endearing desire for love that is the arrival of a new life.

And so, this desire made you full of light with that bell-like smile, and that's how you taught us parents, who had children after you, how to put on diapers, what the best milk is, what potty training is like . . .

Today you don't need a princess costume; you rule, divine among the great ones, the little ones, the butterflies, and the flowers.

Always yours,
Tía Leo

Emma, the most desired girl,

If it weren't for the fact that your birth was envisioned, thought out, and planned by your parents, it could be said that it's a mysterious gift, that you're some prodigy who has come to fulfill her destiny with a magic wand, transforming the lives of those who love her.

Because you are a privileged being touched by grace, nothing in you is ordinary. The decision to look for you—a decision so radical that, although I consider myself a transcendent, even I didn't fully understand it at first—was an immeasurable act of love.

From when you were just a wish in your dads' minds until the moment you arrived, the adventure was guided by that love and absolute dedication. Beautiful and cheerful Emma, who already shows signs of a charming personality, you will be a dancer, actress, or writer, archaeologist or scientist, always adored and pampered in the maelstrom of existence.

When you are old enough to read this letter and the book where your father narrates the extraordinary feat of your birth, perhaps, with your usual curiosity, you will ask him what "maelstrom" means, and remember a distant aunt who keeps you in her mind and spirit.

Tía Norma Niurka

Emma, my Elekemele,

To explain why I consider you my Elekemele instead of Emma, I would have to write you more than one letter, but I'll try to consolidate it in these lines:

I know we don't see each other often, but you are always present, even though you live in the Big Apple and I live in the city of taquitos and the Palacio de Hierro. The only thing I can tell you is that Elekemele is the language with which I can show my affection and thank you. Before you arrived, in my life there were only two little people who made me believe that the impossible could come true: Alacalá and Putumayo, my nieces.

As soon as they were born and I saw them, I knew that those would be the names by which I would recognize them (the names their parents gave them are Carla and Isabel).

A while after their arrival, your parents gave me the news that you were on your way after years and years of searching for you. So when I learned about all the tribulations they went through to get to you, I knew that you too would be another wonderful human being who would make me understand that no matter how complicated it may seem, hope, love, and happiness can be achieved, so I called you Elekemele.

The first time I saw you, you were still in Mary's womb and you were moving inside her under the "Summertime" melody sung by Caetano Veloso, in a video your dad made of you. I will never forget how that CD came into my hands. It was one of the many times that your parents gave me refuge in your house in Miami. Dressed in his Adidas pants and blue Lacoste T-shirt, your dad was sitting in front of the computer in his study overflowing with papers, magazines, and books, and, proudly, with an expression I had never seen on him, he showed me your first pictures and gave me the video. He looked so happy that from that moment on, I thanked you.

Thank you, Elekemele, for enlightening and giving so much life to one of the people who occupies a big piece of my heart. You are very fortunate to be your parents' light, two extraordinary people who, as complicated as it may be, struggle to achieve their dreams and try to understand the "Afrikaner" dialect.

Your aunt Carole

My dear Emma,

I have a very, very clear memory of the day I met you. You were on your parents' table, wrapped up in cloths that looked incredibly cozy, with the entire family gang focused on you. They were all gazing at you, smiling, ecstatic with a happiness that I perceived from the outside in awe. You were everyone's center of the universe. You brought so much happiness! What a privilege to witness your parents' act of magic!

Not in my most surreal dreams could I have imagined that a few years later you would be my Tata, snuggling with us while you sleep, that I would bathe you and untangle your hair and we would laugh together at Sam's incredible IQ . . .

Life takes so many turns, Tata! You continue to give everyone who surrounds you so many joys. I already look up at you instead of downward; now you're the one who paints her nails and puts on makeup and decorates her room with colored lights. You're growing up in every way, and I'm excited to witness how you're becoming a woman.

May this joy you have given us double your happiness, Tatica; may you hold on to that creative mischief that defines you. May the colored lights never be lacking in your imagination. And may life continue to surprise me with gifts as beautiful as growing closer together.

I love you dearly!
PASTA!!!

Tía Tata (Tía Yisel)

Emma, my bandit, my girl,
Life changes in a second. Radically. You turned my life around, in the most beautiful way.

Here we are, Papá Mandy and I, with you since that November afternoon when you came out of Mary's womb to forever win our hearts. You were the most beautiful baby. Papá Mandy was very nervous and couldn't stop shedding tears of joy. I didn't want to waste a second without taking your first photos and, at the same time, etching you forever in my memory.

It took me a while to hold you. I told your dad that I was sweaty, but I was actually a little scared. You were perfect, and I was terrified of hurting you, so fragile. It was hard for me to believe that you were already there and that you were ours.

You were our act of magic. At times you would vanish, but we were still there, fighting, calling you by your name, because you had a name before you became a small cell, like the one in the photo of the book that we read every night.

Now I enjoy every minute that I spend with you because I get to see how you're growing up, changing, learning. I love cooking for you, bathing you, teaching you how to ride a scooter and a bicycle, reading to you, and playing house and everything we invent every day.

Emma, you are our creation. You have two dads who love you dearly and who will be with you, always.

Today I hug you and pinch myself to know that I am no longer dreaming. I am the happiest man in the world because I have you.

I adore you,
Papi Gonzalo

My Emma Isabel,

I close my eyes and I can feel that afternoon in San Diego when we met and I held you in my arms for the first time.

Today, I'm proud of you, of your intelligence, of your calm, of your patience, and I can remember every minute by your side. How time has passed, but in my eyes, you are still my baby.

When you were little, you surprised me at night with your witticisms and your special phrases; like when we started drawing and I wanted to draw a portrait of you and you told me, "Paint me with a happy mouth." Or when you dressed up as a Spanish dancer, started tapping your heels, stopped, and said, "Dad, I like Spanish dancing, but I also like dancing in English."

One day after coming back from New Orleans, where I had to spend a weekend working, you looked me in the eye and said, "I don't want you to work anymore." I explained why I had to work and that I also got sad when I was not with you for a weekend. You were scared, tears filled your eyes, and you interrupted me: "Don't be sad, Papá. When you get sad, all you have to do is call me on the phone."

By the time you were three, you already knew about the magical embryo that gradually grew in the womb of Mary, the surrogate mother; the small cell that Karen, the egg donor, contributed; the day I cut the umbilical cord; how I cried with joy when I saw you come into the world.

I remember back then, at bedtime, while we were leafing through the legends of princesses and enchanted animals, you asked me to also read "In Search of Emma" to you. We'd read that little book of photographs together and you'd hug me before falling asleep and whisper in my ear, as if you wanted to entrust me with a great secret, "Dad, this is my favorite book." And in that moment, I was the happiest dad in the world.

> I love you, with all my heart,
> Your papá Mandy

My dear Anna and Lucas,

Thank you, because your souls decided to live this life experience in our family.

I remember the exact moment, place, and hour when Papá (my son) called me to tell me that you were about to be born. The excitement was endless.

When I had the opportunity to go to San Diego to see you, it was truly an experience of inner joy and pleasure. You were beautiful.

Seeing you both finally among us, your first smiles, your tears, filled me with a deep feeling of gratitude toward life.

This abuelita is very proud of you. Know that you fill my life with love.

> Abuelita Niurca

My Anna,

When you came into the world we had the whole night to ourselves. You were so small and at the same time so firm, with those curious, attentive eyes, always searching for an answer, that from that day on, I began to learn from you. You have come to complete me. We are never born with all the parts we need. You were.

While I was praying for your brother's health, still far from me in that hospital room, we talked about our family, our dreams, the books I wanted to write, the future, and for a moment, I could picture you as an adult. We began a dialogue that to this day is the one we have before falling asleep.

You have no idea how I long for nighttime to come so that you can ask me how my day went and I can tell you every detail until you ask me to ask you "questiones." And there you start that diary of yours that never ceases to amaze me.

You are an old soul. You came to us with a wisdom that is acquired only through the years, one that some never attain.

Let's keep dreaming together. Thank you for giving me the opportunity to continue learning by your side.

You are my life.

All my love to you,
Your Papá

My Lucas,

I've seen you struggle since you were born. You were big and strong, I knew it; and when I got to the hospital you had decided to arrive early. There you were, hooked up to tubes and needles, trying to get your lungs to fill with oxygen.

I saw you through a window, unable to touch you, caress you, embrace you for the first time.

Those were endless days by your side yet separated, until they gave me the opportunity to hold you. That day, I saw you smile for the first time. Maybe it was a simple gesture, an instinctive reaction, but I felt it meant that you recognized me. That you knew I was by your side, always with you, together in battle.

You are the balance in the family. You know how to give and receive a lot of love. And like your sisters, you are smart and wise.

You bear our names, Papi's and mine, and that fills me with pride.

I enjoy watching you grow up, surrounded by friends, admired, and loved.

You are our peace.

Thank you for all your kindness.

Always with you,
Papá

My dear Anna (with two n's),

(I just got your text saying, "Hi.") Reading you always makes my heart leap with joy.

They say that family or friends who are with us have been very close to us in previous lives. I love that idea. I can tell you that since I heard the stories of "Ana" for the first time, I knew that we would be accomplices, that we would understand each other without many words, that I would love meeting you. They told me about your curious gaze, your intuition, your careful nature, recognizing your vulnerabilities and powers beyond the physical ones. So before I saw you for the first time, I met you in stories.

One day it turned out that the girl in the stories became my little niece, and since I met you, I've felt like I knew your soul from before. What are the chances of having two little nieces with the same name? Then I found out about your middle name: Lucía.

Having you close has been an infusion of life from the first day, when you approached me cautiously yet confidently: "Do you want to play with me?" You were sure I'd say yes.

*Since then I look forward to our time together. The games have changed along the way. They were first in Spanish, because you didn't know English, or how to read or write it; then you didn't want **anything** in Spanish. That's when we created your first email: "doglovera" and you were very upset when I wrote "Ana." In a deafening scream: TWO NNNNNN's!!!! Tía Sahi and I bent over laughing. That day I learned that my youngest niece was called "Anna" (with two n's).*

When you grow up, I want you to know about my favorite moments with you, Tata—the ones that I will always cherish, and that make me smile every time they appear . . . Our PJ parties with your sleep-time blankie; putting you in "el shower" and soaking you and your clothes while you scream outrageously; curling up to watch TV before going to bed; when you lie on top of me and hold my hand during movies; seeing your face when I pretend I want to choke you if you push or squeeze me with that herculean strength—a strength I don't I know where you get from— observing your insatiable curiosity when you brush Tara's teeth; gradually discovering your sensitivity and how you try to hide it, as if protecting it; learning to read everything you don't say but feel; seeing your half-smiling, half-disgusted face when I squeeze you and kiss you; amazing me more and more with how you read so easily—not just books, but every moment that surrounds you—with so much skill. Your phrases crack me up: Stop, I'm booored! Tell me a story! Diooos míoooo! *There are so many that they don't fit on this page.*

Our time together has evolved, but it still carries echoes of the first time. It's still a challenge to steal a hug upon arrival (this last time we did it immediately); our stories must be more and more incredible, more politically incorrect, or more hyper-realistic, because the ordinary bores you. You are still as sure of what you want and what you will achieve as the first time you came to play with me. Hopefully, when you read this letter, you'll receive at least a little of the great love that I have for you in my heart . . . infinite!

I'm waiting to see you at our next reunion to continue our last conversation about the meaning of life, as Tía Sahi and I will always be waiting for your texts and your FaceTimes, your laughter, and your unique comments, your embrace, and your always warm little hand.

I love you very much, my Tatica, my Anna (with two n's)!

Tía Tata (Tía Yisel)

My Lucas, my only Titi,

I have enjoyed this task of writing to you almost as much as your embrace.

Do you know how wonderful it is to write things that we feel and don't usually say? We should make up a game the next time we have a sleepover. :)

I want to tell you a story. This one isn't made up like the ones we share in the car. This is one is real . . .

When we met, you were four years old and I was very happy because you became my eldest little nephew. You'd look at me with curiosity between pauses in our conversations with imaginary friends and battles of armies with little soldiers. You asked questions that stole my heart because of their naïveté and candor. You had a lot of Legos, and when I was little I always wanted to have a lot of Legos like yours, so I loved playing with you and building strange things that you later destroyed in a second (or that were destroyed by some "Tatas"). How awful!

Loving you was as natural as your hug. You loved to make up stories and play "I spy." I loved seeing you laugh out loud at the incredible and weird stories I was telling you. It took you a couple of years to decide, but you were the first of the two of you to want to come over to our house for your first sleepover. Tía Sahi and I were bursting with joy! They never told us, but I suspect you were the one who convinced Anna. I'll never forget that day. We had dinner in the living room to celebrate the occasion and toasted with fake champagne! We laughed a lot about the monster that possessed you when dawn fell and you started to let out terrifying screams; we watched movies until very late and you loved that I washed your feet before going to bed. We all slept snuggly in the room, happy.

Titi, you're already getting big and you beat us all at Rummikub. You're enormous, and those gorgeous hands are already almost the size of mine. Who knows what event will come in tow with the next letter that I write to you? While that next letter arrives, I'll write a wish like the ones we burn at the end of the year to make them part of the universe: May you always have your smile, your inner child, the fun and liberating cry at dawn, and the unique and healing hug that you give me each time we meet.

I love you dearly,
Tía Tata (Tía Yisel)

Anna of my heart,

On that wonderful day you and Lucas arrived, we all went to meet you in San Diego—your uncles and aunts, your abuelita Niurca, your cousin Leonorcita, your cousin Fabi. That's why when people asked Emma where she was from, she'd say: "I'm Sandieguera."

You had a mischievous look, observing every movement of those geometric figures, which is how you saw us then because newborn babies see only shapes. You always smiled, very convinced by our craziness and outbursts of contentment.

I will keep our moments in a sacred box:

- *Playing "peo peo."*
- *When you did yoga for the first time at my home, and it was like you'd done it all your life.*
- *Watching movies in your aunts' house, eating popcorn.*
- *Playing hide-and-seek in the country house.*
- *Your scary tales of the dentist when they removed your tooth.*
- *When Tata taught you how to brush Sam's teeth.*
- *When you washed your feet before going to sleep and laughed out loud.*

· *Asking Alexa to tell you stories before going to bed on the floor.*
· *When you bathed on the patio and it got dark, and you didn't stop jumping and laughing in the pool, going around in circles to make waves.*
· *When you learned how to play Rummikub.*
· *Playing Mafia, Pasta, which we so enjoy.*
· *Lighting the December 31 fire to say goodbye to 2019 in the country house and burn our wishes.*
· *And Tayo and Taya's wedding, because Tayo surprised her the same day you were baptized and told Taya the most beautiful words a bride would dream of hearing. It was so moving, we all cried. You should ask Tayo to tell you about it.*

Our little box will have no bottom—it will be infinite like the sky— and there we will continue to save our moments, those that come to stay, with shooting stars, comets, and even planets, and we will always, always, make sure it has plenty of light.

I love you, Anna, and my happiness multiplies with your smile, your FaceTime calls, your messages. With your laughter, your questions, and your games.

I want to finish my letter for you; playing hide-and-seek, I'll stay behind and go searching for you . . . I almost found you . . .

Your happy tía,
Sahi

My great little Lucas,
Since you were in Mary's tummy, you were a restless baby. You rushed out because you knew all too well the happiness and love that awaited you. You did give us a scare. I saw how Papá and Papi, with their eyes, told you how much love there was to give you.

With the birth of your cousin Catherine today, January 9, 2020, my heart remembers similar feelings to the arrival of Emma and the two of you, the first twins in this family. I felt a burst of joy with your early smile, with your little hands that got tangled in devices that made you breathe better and that Papá pushed aside when he gave you milk.

Do you know that you were the biggest, strongest, and most beautiful baby in the NICU nursery?

I remember how the nurse asked Papá and Papi for some of their used clothes to put in your crib so you could smell them.

There are so many moments that are happening today like in a movie. I remember how your parents would put you on top of them so you could feel their warmth. Now more than ever, you are still our big baby.

There's something I've never told you: one of the things I like most in the world is to build Legos with you.

I am your godmother aunt, the happiest one in the world. I'll keep your embrace, just like Fabi's hug, and take it with me, to always hold you near.

I love you with all the strength of my heart.

Your happy madrina tía,
Sahi

Anna,

It seemed like you were going to be a very good girl, but you are tremendous. It seemed like you were only going to be into dolls, and instead you like the ugliest critters, frogs, mice. It seemed like you were going to be a crybaby because you let out some devilish screams and turned tomato red, yet what you like most isn't screaming but giving orders. It seemed like you didn't eat anything because you were small and skinny, but you eat more than a grown man.

With you one never knows what will happen. One thing becomes another. You bring along a surprise each time I see you.

That's why I love being your aunt and your godmother.

Kisses,
Taya

My dear Anna,

Just a brief note to comment on the issue concerning your gift for creating nicknames.

A few years ago, maybe four, you came up with your own private nickname for me, your uncle Néstor. The word chosen by you was Tayo. And as an extension of that, my wife, your dear aunt Esther María, became Taya.

In a flash, the linguistic and logical subtleties of such a wonderful verbal invention became apparent to us: tayo is tío (uncle) in Spanish, but tweaked and tricked by the exchange of the Spanish i (ee) for the English i (ÿ).

As a result, we became your auntie and uncle not only in both English and Spanish, but in some sort of dialect that I would like to call "correacted Spanglish" (after your last name Correa, of course).

When you acted upon the word "tío" and transformed it into "tayo," you "correacted" it. And I'd say that you operated upon the meaning and morphology of that word in such a way as to transform it into something much lovelier and endearing than its original connotation.

Finally, please be advised that, as wordsmiths in our own right, Esther María and I welcome you to the trade and approve of your linguistic experiment in the case of Tayo and Taya.

> *Big hugs and kisses,*
> *Tayo Néstor*

ACKNOWLEDGMENTS

To MY MOTHER, NIURCA; to my sister, Sahily; to my nephew, Fabián; aunts and uncles Leonor, Marisela, Fabrizio, Osvaldo, Néstor, Yisel, Marlén, Ibis, and Ana; to grandparents Esther, Gonzalo, Correa, and Lydia; to cousins Iliana, Ovidio, Romy, Gustavo, Betsy, and Ulises; to Yolanda, Estradelia, Tania, Reizel, María Julia, Nora, Vicky, and Vivian, for joining us on this odyssey.

To my friends and the *People en Español* team, for being patient with my obsessions, especially Chiara, María, Nicole, Ángel, Isis, Miguel, Kika, Elvis, and Carole, who lived through my tribulations to become a dad.

To María Antonieta Collins, Laura García, and Norma Niurka, for encouraging me to write *In Search of Emma*.

To Mirta Ojito, for her wise advice.

To Tía Esther María, for having the patience and dedication to read these pages for the first time.

To the publisher Rene Alegría, for passionately believing in this project and opening the doors for me to make it a reality ten years ago.

To Cecilia Molinari, for her precision as editor ten years ago, and now for the exquisite translation into English.

To the editor Patricia Mazón, who published it in Mexico.

To Omar Cruz, the best photographer, for his incredible patience with Emma, and for the beautiful images he took for the cover of this book.

To Herman Vega, for selecting the best photo and designing the cover.

To the publisher Judith Curr and editor Edward Benítez, for rescuing *In Search of Emma* and giving it the chance to reach a wider audience.

To Johanna Castillo, my friend, editor, and now literary agent, for always believing in me. When you read *In Search of Emma*, you asked me to write a novel and we started a journey together. That's where *The German Girl* came from.

To Becky, who paved the way for me to get to the gestational mothers' agency.

To Greg, father of twins, whose footsteps I followed to find Emma.

To Diana and Melinda from Surrogate Alternatives, who put me in touch with Mary, the gestational mother.

To Darlenne and Becca from A Perfect Match, who facilitated our finding of the egg donor.

To doctors Samuel Wood, Linda Anderson, and Catharine Adams, true geniuses behind the then Reproductive Sciences Center, who helped me create Emma, as well as their entire team, especially Angela Scroop and Suham Rojas.

To attorney Thomas Pinkerton and his team, for helping me navigate intricate legal loopholes.

To Dr. Hamilton Steele, who brought Emma, Anna, and Lucas into the world.

To Dr. Lisa Pérez-Grossman, for being a friend and for helping us with Emma from the day she was born. To her entire team, for their dedication, especially Lianet.

To the egg donor, for having contributed the necessary half to create Emma, Anna, and Lucas.

To Mary, for her kindness and tenderness; for having incubated Emma, Anna, and Lucas during nine months.

To Gonzalo, because together we searched for and found Emma, Anna, and Lucas.

BIBLIOGRAPHY

Adams, Catharine A., Linda S. Anderson, Angela L. Scroop, Samuel H. Wood. "Gestational Surrogacy Enhances Implantation Rates in Egg Donation Cycles." *Fertility and Sterility* (a journal of the American Society for Reproductive Medicine) 80, suppl. 3 (September 2003): 135.

Beck, Melinda. "Ova Time: Women Line Up to Donate Eggs for Money." *Wall Street Journal*, December 9, 2008.

Crook, Hank, and Tom Fudge. "A Growing Number of Military Wives Are Becoming Surrogate Mothers." *These Days on KPBS*, July 14, 2009.

Darrach, Brad. "Baby M." *People*, October 4, 1989.

Derek, Julia. *Confessions of a Serial Egg Donor*. Adrenaline Books, 2004.

Didion, Joan. *The Year of Magical Thinking*. Vintage International, 2007.

Dutton, Gail. *A Matter of Trust: The Guide to Gestational Surrogacy*. Clouds Publishing, 1997.

Ehrensaft, Diane. *Mommies, Daddies, Donors, Surrogates: Answering Tough Questions and Building Strong Families*. Guilford Press, 2005.

Fassa, Lynda. *Green Kids, Sage Families: The Ultimate Guide to Raising Your Organic Kids*. New American Library, 2009.

Fenton-Glynn, Claire. "Surrogacy: Why the World Needs Rules for 'Selling' Babies." *BBC News*, April 26, 2019.

Fleming, Nic. "Scientist Makes Clone of Himself from Skin Cells." *Telegraph*, January 18, 2008.

Green, Ronald M. *Babies by Design: The Ethics of Genetic Choice*. Yale University Press, 2007.

Griswold, Zara. *Surrogacy Was the Way: Twenty Intended Mothers Tell Their Stories*. Nightingale Press, 2005.

Haberman, Clyde. "Baby M and the Question of Surrogate Motherhood." Retro Report. *New York Times*, March 23, 2014.

Hartman, Kendra. "La Jolla Doctor Sees the Potential in Every Infertility Case." San Diego Community Newspaper Group, December 9, 2013. http://sdnews.com/view/full_story/24191613/article-La-Jolla-doctor-sees-the-potential-in-every-infertility-case?instance=sdnews_business_page.

Hornblower, Margot. "Judge Awards 'Baby M' to her Biological Father." *Washington Post*, April 1, 1987.

"In the Matter of Baby M., a Pseudonym for an Actual Person." Supreme Court of New Jersey. 109 N.J. 396 (1988); 537 A.2d 1227. https://law.justia.com/cases/new-jersey/supreme-court/1988/109-n-j-396-1.html.

Kane, Elizabeth. *Birth Mother: The Courageous, Intimate Story of America's First Surrogate Mother*. Harcourt Brace Jovanovich, 1988.

Kane, Elizabeth. "Surrogate Mother Elizabeth Kane Delivers Her 'Gift of Love'—Then Kisses Her Baby Goodbye." *People*, December 8, 1980.

Lewin, Tamar. "Egg Donors Challenge Pay Rates, Saying They Shortchange Women." *New York Times*, October 16, 2015.

Lewis Cooper, Susan, and Ellen Sarasohn Glazer. *Choosing Assisted Reproduction: Social, Emotional and Ethical Considerations*. Perspectives Press, 1998.

Markens, Susan. *Surrogate Motherhood and the Politics of Reproduction*. Univ. of California Press, 2007.

Mazziotta, Julie. "How a Trailblazer in Surrogacy and Sperm and Egg Donation Helped Thousands Become Parents." *People* Online, May 1, 2019. https://people.com/health/doctor-became -surrogacy-expert/.

Menichiello, Michael. *A Gay Couple's Journey Through Surrogacy: Intended Fathers*. Haworth Press, 2006.

Mundy, Liza. *Everything Conceivable: How Assisted Reproduction Is Changing Our World*. Anchor Books, 2007.

O'Neill, Anne-Marie, and Susan Schindehette. "The Hendersons: A Single Father Through Surrogacy." *People*, May, 15, 2000.

Orenstein, Peggy. *Waiting for Daisy: The True Story of One Couple's Quest to Have a Baby*. Bloomsbury, 2008.

Pollitt, Katha. "The Strange Case of Baby M." *The Nation*, January 2, 1998. https://www.thenation.com/article/archive/strange-case -baby-m/.

Ragoné, Helena. *Surrogate Motherhood: Conception in the Heart*. Westview Press, 1994.

Salkin, Allen. "She's Come a Long Way, Baby M: Gifted Child Born Amid a Two-Family Uproar Thrives." *New York Post*, March 21, 1999.

Sandel, Michael J. *The Case Against Perfection: Ethics in the Age of Genetic Engineering*. Belknap Press, 2007.

Sarasohn Glazer, Ellen, and Evelina Weidman Sterling. *Having Your Baby Through Egg Donation*. Perspectives Press, 2005.

Shaughnessy, Mary. "All for Love of a Baby." *People*, March 23, 1987.

Sills, E. Scott, and others. "Gestational Surrogacy and the Role of Routine Embryo Screening: Current Challenges and Future Directions for Preimplantation Genetic Testing." Wiley Online Library, November 23, 2015. https://pubmed.ncbi.nlm.nih.gov/26598285/.

Stotland, Nada L. *Psychiatric Aspects of Reproductive Technology.* American Psychiatric Press, 1990.

Telling, Gillian. "Four Surrogates Share Why They Carried Babies for Other Families—and Whether They'd Do It Again." *People* Online, October 24, 2019. https://people.com/human-interest/4-surrogates-share-why-they-carried-babies-for-others/.

"Thomas Pinkerton: The San Diego Surrogacy Case." CNN Community, August 15, 2001. http://www.cnn.com/2001/COMMUNITY/08/15/pinkerton/.

Vilar, Irene. *Impossible Motherhood: Testimony of an Abortion Addict.* Other Press, 2009.

Watson Rapley, Sandra. *Intended Parents: Miracle Do Happen—A True-Life Success Story of Having Children Through Surrogacy.* iUniverse, 2005.

Whitehead, Mary Beth. *A Mother's Story: The Truth About the Baby M Case.* St. Martin's Press, 1989.

Whitehead, Mary Beth. "A Surrogate Mother Describes Her Change of Heart—and Her Fight to Keep the Baby Two Families Love." *People*, October 20, 1986.

Ziegler, Stacy. *Pathways to Parenthood: The Ultimate Guide to Surrogacy.* Brown Walker Press, 2005.